REDCAR & CLEVELAND COLLEGE LIBRARY

CYTHDRAWN
218123

00034739
551

P

UNDERSTANDING THE PHYSICAL WORLD

are to be returned on or before
date below

KU-508-309

IAN GALBRAITH

OXFORD UNIVERSITY PRESS

REDCAR & CLEVELAND COLLEGE LIBRARY

80 9/15

Oxford University Press, Great Clarendon Street, Oxford OX2 6DP

Oxford New York
Athens Auckland Bangkok Bogota Bombay
Buenos Aires Calcutta Cape Town Dar es Salaam
Delhi Florence Hong Kong Istanbul Karachi
Kuala Lumpur Madras Madrid Melbourne
Mexico City Nairobi Paris Singapore
Taipei Tokyo Toronto

and associated companies in
Berlin Ibadan

Oxford is a trademark of Oxford University Press

© Oxford University Press 1995

First published 1995
Reprinted 1997

ISBN 0 19 913388 3

All rights reserved. No part of this publication may be produced, stored in a retrieval system, or transmitted, in any form or by any means, without the prior permission in writing of Oxford University Press. Within the UK, exceptions are allowed in respect of any fair dealing for the purpose of research or private study, or criticism or review, as permitted under the Copyright, Designs and Patents Act, 1988, or in the case of reprographic reproduction in accordance with the terms of licences issued by the Copyright Licensing Agency. Enquiries concerning reproduction outside those terms and in other countries should be sent to the Rights Department, Oxford University Press, at the address above.

Printed in Hong Kong

P This symbol in the text denotes a *practical exercise*.

We hope you will find this book useful if you are working for your GCSE and also that it will encourage you to look more closely at the world around you. Wherever you live or travel, the earth's surface provides varied scenery which becomes more interesting if you understand how it was formed and why it varies from place to place. Ideally you should study the landscape at first hand, but unfortunately opportunities for field work are always limited. Photographs and diagrams are the next best thing – careful study of the illustrations is just as important as reading the words in between!

Contents

1 Landforms and landscapes

Fig. 1 A landscape made up of landforms: Snowdonia

Look at the photograph (Fig. 1) of Snowdonia. This impressive *landscape* is made up of *landforms* such as mountain peaks, ridges and lakes. Other landforms, not shown here, include volcanoes, waterfalls, cliffs, and sand dunes. Landscapes are made up from different combinations of landforms.

The science that studies landforms is called *geomorphology*. Geomorphologists are interested in the shape of landforms, the processes that make them the shape they are, and how their shape has changed through time.

1 Describe the landscape of your home area. If you live in a town, try to describe the shape of the land on which the town is built. You should be able to identify hills and valleys even if they are covered by buildings. You may find it helpful to refer to the contours on a local Ordnance Survey map.

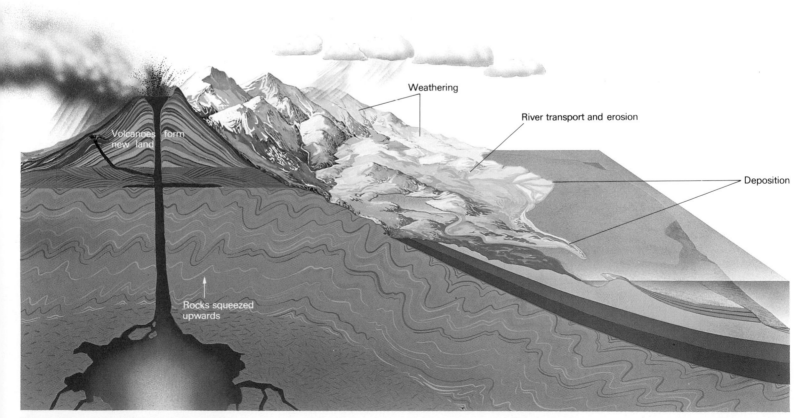

Fig. 2 Mountain building and denudation

Landform processes

A *process* is a series of events or changes. Landscapes are the result of two major sets of processes acting on the surface of the earth (Fig. 2).

Firstly, there are those processes which add new material to the earth's crust or which cause it to be uplifted. These include the flow of molten lava from volcanoes, and large-scale earth movements. We may call these the processes of *mountain building*.

Secondly, there are those processes which destroy or wear away the rocks and landforms of the earth's surface. These are called the processes of *denudation*.

Rocks on the earth's surface are in contact with the atmosphere and the oceans and it is water that is mostly responsible for denudation. Rainwater causes rocks to decay, valleys are cut by running water and by glacier ice, and the coast is worn away by the action of waves. It is easier to understand denudation if we see it as the result of several distinct processes.

Weathering is the breakdown of rocks at or near the surface of the earth. This word is used because it is the weather that is mainly responsible. Some minerals in rocks, for example, are dissolved by rainwater which causes the rock to crumble.

Rock waste, broken up by weathering, does not remain in the same position for very long. Rivers, glaciers, the sea, and winds carry weathered fragments away. This is called *transportation*. Transportation may also be a direct result of gravity. This occurs when weathered fragments roll downhill or fall from a cliff face. Material moved by all these processes may be large boulders of solid rock or tiny particles dissolved in water.

The word *erosion* refers to the cutting and shaping of the earth's surface. Think of a sculptor carving a statue. A chisel is used to break off pieces of wood or stone. These pieces fall to the floor by gravity. In the landscape, running water, the sea, moving ice, and wind act as chisels. They transport rock fragments and also use these fragments to wear away the landscape. Pebbles at the bottom of a cliff, for

Fig. 3 A stream table

example, are transported by the waves, but they may also be hurled at the cliff in stormy seas, eroding it.

All transported rock particles eventually settle. This is called *deposition*. Rivers deposit fine silt and mud in the sea, sometimes as deltas. Similarly, glacier ice dumps the rocks it carries when the ice melts. The rocks broken off crags pile up in heaps at the foot of the mountainside.

If conditions stay the same for long enough these deposits may become compressed by the weight of more deposits on top. Eventually this results in new rock being formed.

One way of learning more about the processes at work on landscape is by making models. The picture above shows a *stream table*. This is a large tray filled with sand. Water squirted through a jet flows across the sand and behaves like a river. This smaller version of a river allows us to simplify the real river so that we can understand the basic processes at work.

Another way of helping us to understand processes in geomorphology is by thinking of them as *systems*. Think of the appliances that use water in your home. The sink, bath, w.c. and so on are all separate, but you cannot really understand how they work unless you think of them all being linked together. Figure 4 shows the water system of a house. To keep the diagram simple, only the cold water is shown. Notice that the system depends on a flow through the pipes in the house. Pure water going into the house is called the *input* and the waste water is called the *output*. The system also includes *stores* such as the water tank.

Systems can be of different sizes. One of the smallest water systems in a house might be a sink. Input is through the taps and output through the waste pipe. The

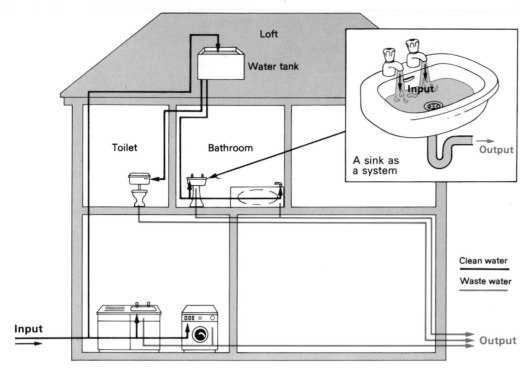

Fig. 4 A water system in the home

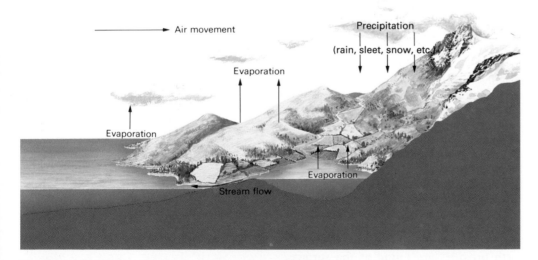

Fig. 5 The hydrological cycle: the biggest water system

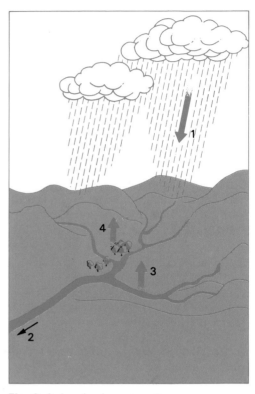

Fig. 6 A river basin as a system

the mountains by the movement of air from the sea towards the land. Water vapour is further cooled and the droplets of water collect together to form rain. Rivers are fed by rainfall and return water to the sea.

---

2 a Discuss the meaning of the following terms: *evaporation, condensation, precipitation*. Write a definition for each.
b Draw a simplified version of Fig. 5 to show the hydrological cycle. Add labels to describe what is happening.

The hydrological cycle is a very large system. It represents the movement of all the water on the earth. There are no inputs or outputs, as all the water in the world is

water system diagram helps us to understand how the water supply in a home works. We can understand how the landscape works by drawing similar system diagrams.

Figure 5 shows the largest water system of all – the *hydrological* (or *water*) *cycle*. This is how it works. Water vapour evaporates from the sea. As it rises it condenses to form clouds. Clouds are forced to rise over

recirculated within the cycle. Systems in the landscape are not all large, however. We could look at a river basin as a smaller part of the larger system (like the sink in the house). A river basin has an input of water from rainfall and an output of water along the river and by evaporation.

---

3 a Make a simple copy of Fig. 6. Label the arrows showing the movement of water and say whether each is an input or an output.
b State two ways in which water may be stored in a natural river basin.

Systems like this help us to simplify the real world in the same way as the stream table does. For this reason we can also call systems *models*.

Time

Consider a large cathedral such as Canterbury or St Paul's. During its long history it may have been altered from its original style and shape. Some parts have worn down slowly through age or have been destroyed suddenly in wartime. Builders throughout history have added new parts to the original building, perhaps in different styles or using different materials. The building we see today is therefore the result of a series of changes in its history. The landscape is like this, only more complex. This is partly because it has had a much longer history – perhaps 500 million years compared with one thousand years for the cathedral. Time is, therefore, an important aspect of the study of geomorphology. Many of the processes operating on the surface of the earth are very slow, so it is not surprising that people used to think of the landscape as unchanging – the hills and valleys were seen as 'everlasting'.

We now know that a great many changes have taken place in the past to explain the present landscape and that these changes, however gradual, are continuing today. The position of land and sea has altered many times and the climate has also changed. The present landscape of Britain is only temporary.

Geomorphology and people

Why should we study geomorphology? One reason is that people are naturally interested in their surroundings. Every year, more people spend their leisure time in the countryside and they want to understand the scenery they enjoy. This book shows how landscapes change. Natural changes take place very slowly but modern technology enables people to change the landscape very rapidly indeed. Whole hillsides can be removed to provide stone for building. Deep quarries can be excavated for sand and gravel. Cuttings are made for motorways. The power that people have to change the surface of the earth makes the study of geomorphology more important. Landscapes may need to be *managed* so that their character is kept for the next generation. In some areas, development has been carefully controlled. Many of the natural landscapes of Britain have been partly protected by being designated National Parks, National Nature Reserves, or Sites of Special Scientific Interest.

Geomorphology is not just about enjoying landscapes, though. The natural environment can be a very dangerous place! Studying the processes that cause natural disasters such as landslides or floods can save lives. Geomorphologists can do little to prevent volcanoes erupting but the effects of natural hazards can often be reduced. Buildings can be designed to withstand earthquake tremors or the effects of subsidence. Early warnings can be given to people living in areas likely to flood. These measures depend on being able to predict when a disaster will occur.

The physical environment may be seen as a collection of *hazards*, but it is also a *resource*. Some of the useful materials the earth provides are found at the surface, like water and soil. Others are found underground, like coal and metals. Processes on earth are constantly making new resources but these processes are slow, perhaps taking millions of years. Geomorphologists are as interested in the management of the earth's resources as they are in the conservation of landscapes.

---

4 a Make a list of natural disasters. Look through this book for some clues.
b Make a list of 10 useful materials from the earth.

---

2 Rocks and earth movements

Many different rocks make up the crust of the earth. They may be hard like granite, soft like clay, or loose like gravel. There is a great variety of colour, weight, and hardness. It is worth knowing more about the study of rocks in order to understand landforms.

Hard rocks are more resistant to being worn away and so they usually form upland areas. People's lives are directly affected by the rocks beneath their feet. In upland areas communications are more difficult. Roads may be restricted to the valley floors. There are fewer large towns. Soils are thinner and slopes are steeper, and it is often colder and wetter. Farmers do not have a wide choice of crops and livestock.

Lowland areas of softer rocks also have their problems. Loose sands and gravels may provide building materials but the buildings require special foundations. Soft clays may cause landslides on slopes and cliffs.

Rocks are usually grouped into three types, depending on how they were formed. These three groups are:

- the *igneous* rocks
- the *sedimentary* rocks
- the *metamorphic* rocks.

The relationship between these three rock types may be seen below. This diagram shows a system called the *geological cycle*. Remember that it takes millions of years for the materials that make up the crust of the earth to pass through this cycle.

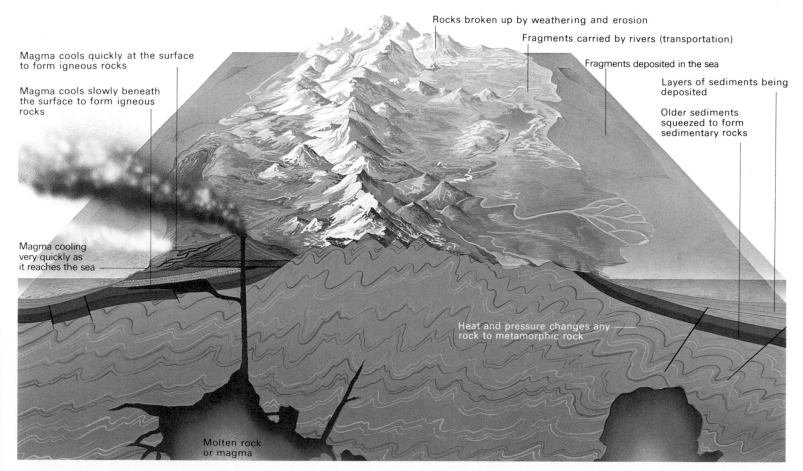

Magma cools quickly at the surface to form igneous rocks

Magma cools slowly beneath the surface to form igneous rocks

Magma cooling very quickly as it reaches the sea

Molten rock or magma

Rocks broken up by weathering and erosion

Fragments carried by rivers (transportation)

Fragments deposited in the sea

Layers of sediments being deposited

Older sediments squeezed to form sedimentary rocks

Heat and pressure changes any rock to metamorphic rock

Fig. 1 Another system: the geological cycle

Igneous rocks

These are rocks that have cooled from the hot liquid or *magma* beneath the crust of the earth. If movements take place in the crust this magma may push upwards and spill out onto the surface as volcanoes or lava flows. As the magma cools, *crystals* grow and igneous rock is formed. Large crystals are formed if the magma cools slowly. Magma that spills out onto the surface cools rapidly and the crystals are small. The smallest crystals of all are found in rocks where the magma has poured into the sea. Some igneous rocks, like volcanic glass, have no crystals at all. Igneous rocks can usually be recognised by their crystals, and individual *minerals* may be especially clearly seen if the magma cooled slowly.

---

1 A geologist has collected two types of igneous rock. To help her examine them she has made a thin slice of each rock and studied these carefully under a microscope. She can then see the minerals clearly. Study Fig. 2, which shows the rocks she has collected. Describe the appearance of these two rocks.

The geologist concludes that rock (a) is *granite* and that rock (b) is *basalt*. If possible study specimens of these rocks. Notice that many of the crystals in basalt are very small. Basalt magma cooled on or near the surface. Granite magma cooled slowly, deep in the earth's crust.

When igneous rocks cool they often shrink and crack. These cracks are known as *joints*. Figure 36 on p. 25 shows the hexagonal pattern of joints that is sometimes found in basalt.

Sedimentary rocks

Rocks at the surface are broken up by the weather. Small particles of rock are often carried away by water, moving ice or wind and deposited somewhere else. The deposited material is called a *sediment*. The most common types of sediment are found under water in the sea. The layers of soft, loose mud and sand that have been de-

Fig. 2 A geologist studying rocks

(a)

(b)

posited by rivers are gradually changed into sedimentary rocks. After many years successive layers of sediment accumulate on the sea floor. Air and water are squeezed out of the lower layers. Often the water that is squeezed out leaves behind chemicals that may cement the grains of mud and sand together. *Sandstone* is a sedimentary rock. Most of the rock is made up of 'sand' or grains of quartz.

2 Study Fig. 3 and, if possible, a piece of sandstone. You may notice that the grains of quartz are more rounded in the sandstone than in granite.

a Can you explain why? Remember where the quartz has come from in each case.

b The hardness of quartz can be compared with the other two minerals in granite (felspar and mica) as follows:

quartz: cannot be scratched with a penknife

felspar: can be scratched with a penknife

mica: can just be scratched with a fingernail.

Consider, from the beginning, how sedimentary rocks are formed. Can you suggest why many of them are made of quartz and not of felspar or mica?

Fig. 3 Sandstone: a sedimentary rock

3 Half fill a glass container with water. Drop a handful of sand into the container and allow it to settle. Drop in another handful of powdered clay and leave to settle for a few days. Repeat the procedure. You will find that layers are settling in the container.

These layers represent different periods of deposition. The layers of rock or *strata* in sedimentary rocks may often be clearly seen, separated by *bedding planes*.

When rocks are deposited, the strata and bedding planes are usually horizontal. Later though, because of movements in the earth's crust, the rocks may be tilted and the strata are then said to *dip*. The angle of dip may be measured easily using a *clinometer*, an instrument rather like a protractor (p. 78).

Sedimentary rocks are often divided into groups according to the size of the

Fig. 4 Shelly limestone

fragments that make them up. *Conglomerate* is made from rounded pebbles. *Clay* is a sedimentary rock with very small grains about 1/250 mm in diameter. *Sandstone* has grains larger than clay but smaller than conglomerate.

Not all sediments, though, are formed from the remains of other rocks. There is a second type of sedimentary rock which consists of the remains of plants or animals or the accumulation of chemicals in water. Where the sea contains more of a chemical than it can dissolve, the surplus is deposited on the sea floor. Calcium carbonate, rock salt, and gypsum are sometimes deposited directly in this way. Calcium carbonate can also be formed by the action of sea creatures in making their shells. When the animals die their shells fall to the sea bed and pile up, often to a great thickness. Masses of shells may then be cemented together, usually by more calcium carbonate. The shells are often clearly seen in the rock (see above). A rock that contains a large amount of calcium carbonate, whether it has been deposited directly or indirectly in the form of shells, is known as a *limestone*.

Fossils are the traces of animals and plants that have been preserved in rocks.

Dead ammonite on the sea floor. These animals are now extinct.

The fleshy parts have now rotted, and the spiral shell is being covered in mud.

The shell is now buried. It may decay and be replaced by a mineral such as calcite.

There are several types of fossil. Firstly, the shell or skeleton of the animal may be preserved as in Fig. 5. Secondly, the shell or skeleton may have left an impression in the mud in which it was deposited. Thirdly, the original plant or animal may have been gradually replaced by some other substance. Often, for example, crystals of a mineral called *calcite* grow in the spaces left by shells that have rotted. Figure 5 shows how a fossil is formed.

---

4 Most fossils are the remains of animals with shells that lived in the sea. Why should this be so?

5 Fossils are only found in sedimentary rocks. Why are there no fossils in igneous rocks?

Not all sedimentary rocks are formed under the sea. New Red Sandstone was formed at a time when much of Britain was a desert, by the cementing together of windblown sand. If you look at New Red Sandstone under a magnifying glass you can see that the small grains of quartz are scratched. This scratching happened as the grains jostled against each other in desert sandstorms.

Metamorphic rocks

Metamorphic rocks have been changed from their original form by heat or by pressure beneath the surface of the earth.

When molten rock, at a temperature of several hundred degrees centigrade, is forced upwards, the surrounding rock becomes baked and hot gases are given off. New minerals and crystals grow and the rock is altered.

Slate is a metamorphic rock which has been formed by the prolonged heating and squeezing of *shale*, a soft sedimentary rock formed by the deposition of mud. Slate splits easily into thin sheets and for this reason has been important as a roofing material. Figure 6 explains why the rock does this.

Fig. 5 The formation of a fossil ammonite

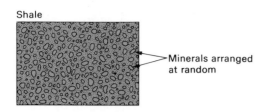

Shale

Minerals arranged at random

Shale is squeezed

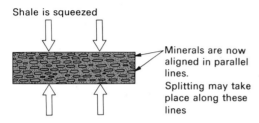

Minerals are now aligned in parallel lines.
Splitting may take place along these lines

Fig. 6 How slate is formed

---

6 Under heat and pressure, limestone becomes *marble* and sandstone becomes *quartzite*.

a What is marble commonly used for?

b Metamorphic rocks are often very hard and resistant to wear. Why should this be so?

c Why are few fossils or bedding planes present in sedimentary rocks that have experienced heat or pressure?

7 Refer to the diagram of the geological cycle (Fig. 1 on p. 9). Make a copy of the diagram and write a paragraph to describe how the cycle works.

Water in rocks

Rocks that allow water to pass through them are called *permeable* rocks. Those, like granite, that will not let water through are *impermeable*. Permeable rocks are of two sorts, *pervious* and *porous*. Pervious rocks have cracks formed by bedding planes and joints. Water seeps through the cracks. Carboniferous limestone is a pervious rock. Porous rocks have air spaces in them like a sponge. Water passes through the pores. Chalk is a soft, white, porous rock.

Earthquake damage

8 a List the damage that resulted from the Californian earthquake of October 1989.

b Imagine an earthquake of this size happening in Britain and affecting cities 300 km away. If it took place in Birmingham, in which other major cities would the shocks be felt?

People who live on the western side of the USA and Canada face the constant threat of earthquakes. When the earth's crust twists and cracks, huge forces are released which are measured on the *Richter scale*. The value of 6.9 (Fig. 7) recorded in California showed that there had been a severe earthquake, though this was not the

Earthquake death toll may be 300

The death toll in northern California rose rapidly towards 300 yesterday as a big rescue operation got under way after the second worst earthquake ever to hit the United States.

Dawn broke over the San Francisco area to reveal collapsed freeways and bridges, raging fires, shattered buildings, landslides and roads criss-crossed by gaping cracks.

Last night estimates were being issued of 273 people dead and 1,400 injured.

At least 253 were feared to have been killed when a mile-long section of supposedly earthquake-proof elevated freeway in Oakland collapsed during the rush hour, crushing cars on the road beneath to a height of a foot or less.

Hospitals were flooded with hundreds of injured. A million or more people were without power and other vital services.

Across the bay in Oakland, rescue workers yesterday called off efforts to find any injured in the collapsed stretch of freeway, known as the Cypress structure.

Troops were ordered onto the streets on Tuesday night by Mr Art Agnos, the San Francisco mayor, after early reports of sporadic looting and vandalism. However, Mr Agnos praised the "sensational" conduct of the city's population in the hours after the earthquake, singling out the way they had helped and cared for each other.

The rolling earthquake along the San Andreas fault, which struck just after 5 pm local time on Tuesday, measured 6.9 on the Richter scale. Its tremors were felt 400 miles away in Los Angeles. There were reports of damage 200 miles away in Reno, Nevada.

Passengers on the first flight to Britain out of San Francisco yesterday described scenes of devastation as the earthquake rocked the city.

Father Keven Doheny of Dublin, who was working on an international campaign for refugees, was leaving his host's house in Menlo Park, south of San Francisco, to drive to the airport when the earthquake struck. He said: "The house began to rock. First, there was a dreadful rumbling noise. It was frightening. We ran out and saw the pool overflowing on the lawn, like a rough sea. Water came into the house, into the bedrooms."

Fig. 7 The California earthquake, October 1989

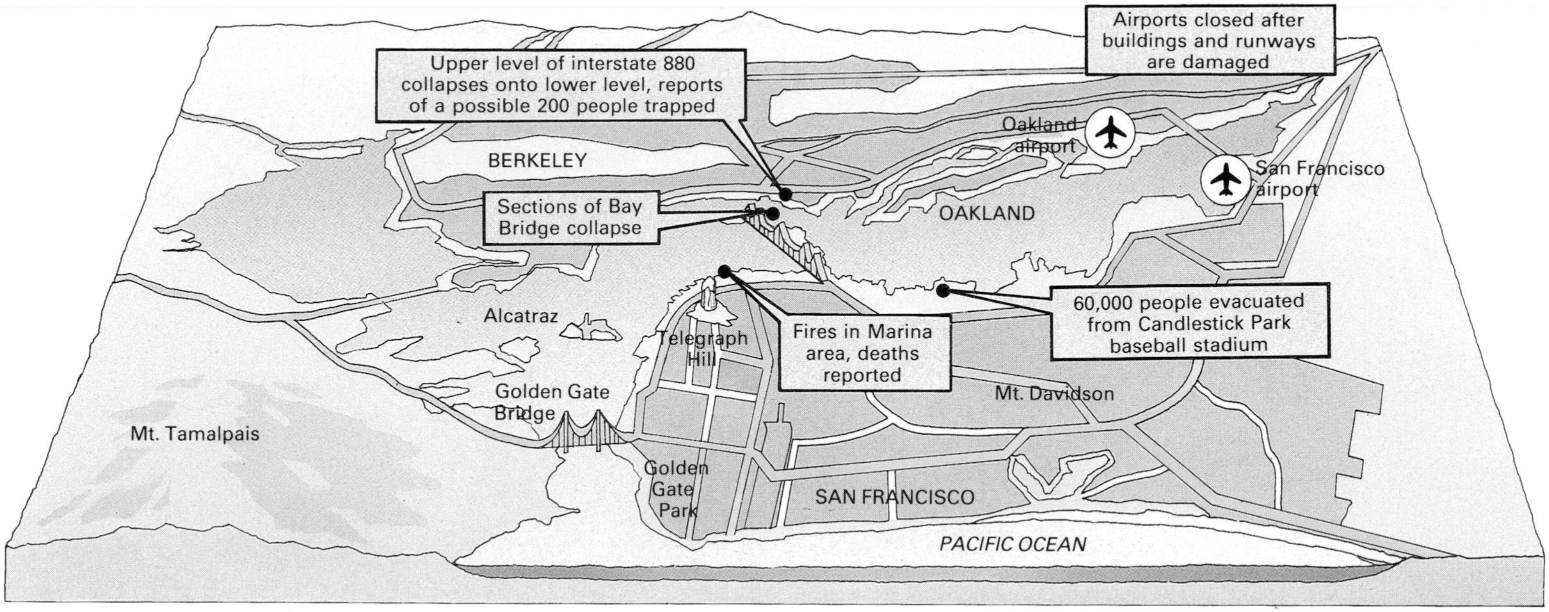
Airports closed after buildings and runways are damaged
Upper level of interstate 880 collapses onto lower level, reports of a possible 200 people trapped
Oakland airport
BERKELEY
San Francisco airport
Sections of Bay Bridge collapse
OAKLAND
60,000 people evacuated from Candlestick Park baseball stadium
Alcatraz
Telegraph Hill
Fires in Marina area, deaths reported
Golden Gate Bridge
Mt. Davidson
Mt. Tamalpais
Golden Gate Park
SAN FRANCISCO
PACIFIC OCEAN

Fig. 8 Block diagram showing events during the 1989 Californian earthquake

worst earthquake ever to hit San Francisco. In 1906, an earthquake measuring 8.3 on the Richter scale led to the loss of over 700 lives in the city.

San Francisco lies near the San Andreas *fault*, a huge series of cracks in the earth's crust. Movement along the fault is continuing and other severe earthquakes can be expected. Buildings in San Francisco are now designed to sway gently when an earthquake strikes, as this makes them less likely to collapse. Unfortunately, the raised section of freeway (motorway) that collapsed in Oakland (Fig. 8) did not include some of the features that would have allowed it to survive the earthquake.

Large sums of money are being spent in efforts to forecast and even control earthquakes. However, the warning signs are very small and the forces released by an earthquake are very powerful. This presents great problems to the scientists and so far they have had only limited success.

Forecasting and controlling earthquakes

Before earthquakes can be controlled, geologists must try to understand why they happen and work out where they are most likely to occur. *Seismologists* specialise in studying earthquakes and have discovered that shocks are associated with the buckling and cracking of rocks at depths of up to 300 km.

Think what happens if you hold a plastic ruler in both hands and gradually bend it. Strains build up until eventually the ruler breaks. Energy stored in the ruler as it was bent is released as shock waves – a cracking noise and vibrations along the broken halves of the ruler. The earth's crust behaves in a similar way. Strains build up until the crust breaks and energy is released in an earthquake.

The point of origin of an earthquake is known as its *focus* (Fig. 10). Shock waves are first felt at the *epicentre*, the place on the earth's surface above the focus, and the worst damage is usually in this area. Several types of wave move outwards from the focus. The first waves to arrive are known as primary (P) waves and these are followed by secondary (S) waves. P and S waves move through the earth but the last waves to arrive travel along the surface. These do the most damage, causing the earth to move both up and down and from side to side. All these waves are picked up and recorded by *seismographs*.

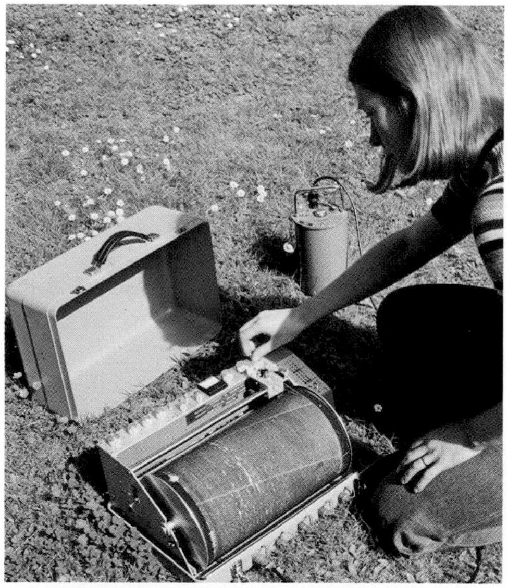

Fig. 9 Recording earthquakes: a seismograph

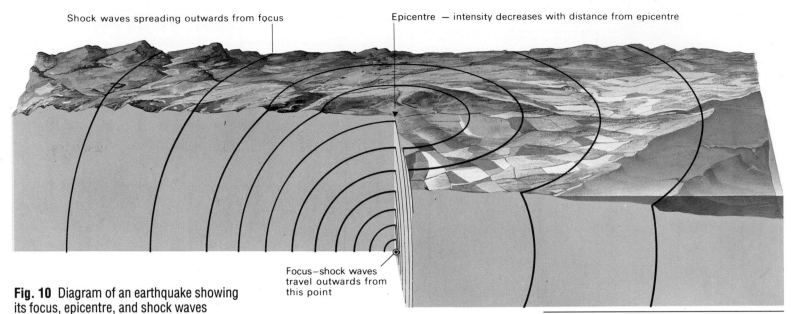

Shock waves spreading outwards from focus

Epicentre — intensity decreases with distance from epicentre

Focus—shock waves travel outwards from this point

Fig. 10 Diagram of an earthquake showing its focus, epicentre, and shock waves

If the records of all the world's seismic stations are put together, it is immediately clear that some areas are greatly at risk from earthquakes. In these danger zones, the rocks are moving and cracking along faults. Earthquake records are used to pinpoint places along fault lines where an earthquake has not happened in recent years and where tensions must be building up. This allows seismologists to say *where* an earthquake is likely. To say *when* it will occur is far more difficult. Some progress towards successful forecasting is being made by studying changes in the rocks which take place immediately before an earthquake, but the days of accurate earthquake prediction are still some way ahead. Meanwhile, scientists are experimenting with ways of controlling earthquakes. If movement along fault lines were to take place as frequent, small jerks rather than a few large movements there would be less risk to life and property. Some success has been achieved by pumping water into the fault zone, which lubricates the fault and allows movement to take place before huge stresses build up. But such experiments are dangerous and are being carried out very cautiously.

9 Study Fig. 11. List 10 cities with a population of one million or more which are in danger zones. (You can find the names of the cities in an atlas.)

Plate tectonics

The structure of the earth

We have seen that earthquakes are associated with movement along faults and that they happen most regularly in particular areas of the world. Looking at Fig. 11, we see that there are narrow zones of earthquake belts which surround large, more stable areas. The geological pattern is repeated if we study maps of major mountain ranges and volcanoes. Figure 11 also shows the world's structural areas. The *shields* are regions of very old rocks where there is little movement. Elsewhere mountains have formed at various periods of the earth's history. The oldest *(Caledonian)* mountains have often been worn down. *Hercynian* earth movements and particularly the more recent *Alpine* movements formed the great mountain ranges of the world today.

10 On tracing paper, copy the outlines of the continents from Fig. 11. Shade the areas of Alpine fold mountains and then use an atlas to help plot the following volcanoes on the same map (several of you could work on the same base map, each plotting a few of the volcanoes in this list):

Vesuvius	41°N 14°E
Mt Hood	45°N 122°W
Etna	38°N 15°E
Paricutin	19°N 102°W
Hekla	64°N 20°W
Santorini	36°N 25°E
Kilimanjaro	3°S 37°E
Villarrica	39°S 72°W
Cotopaxi	1°S 78°W
Ruapehu	39°S 176°E
Krakatoa	6°S 105°E
Mayon	13°N 124°E
Fuji	35°N 138°E
Lassen Peak	40°N 121°W
Mauna Loa	19°N 156°W
Mt Pelée	15°N 61°W
Tenerife	28°N 17°W
Tristan de Cunha	37°S 12°W
Aconcagua	33°S 70°W

Place your tracing over Fig. 11. What do you notice about the location of earthquakes and young fold mountains? How many of the volcanoes are also in these areas?

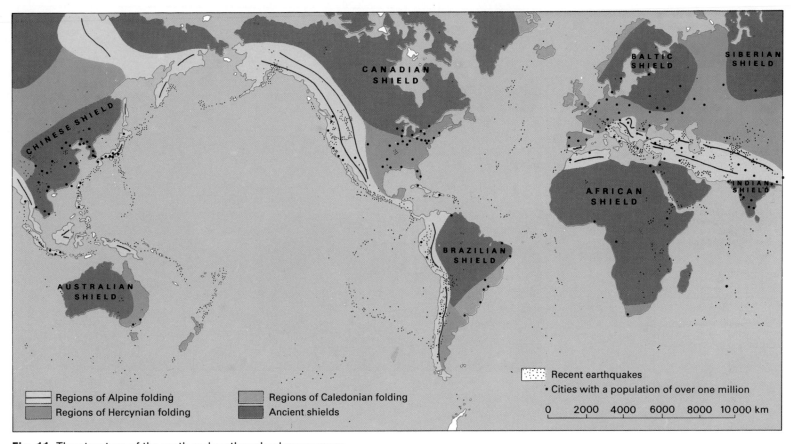

Fig. 11 The structure of the earth and earthquake danger zones

Legend:
- Regions of Alpine folding
- Regions of Hercynian folding
- Regions of Caledonian folding
- Ancient shields
- Recent earthquakes
- • Cities with a population of over one million

Scale: 0 2000 4000 6000 8000 10 000 km

Most of the earthquakes and volcanoes occur in areas of young fold mountains or in the oceans where, as we shall see later, there are underwater mountain ranges as spectacular as those found on the continents. Could this be mere coincidence? Since the 1960s evidence has been collected which helps us explain the connexion between earthquakes, volcanoes, and mountain ranges. The theory of *plate tectonics* is one of the great scientific advances of the twentieth century. It is now accepted by almost all earth scientists, though there are many areas where our understanding of the unstable earth is still incomplete. To follow this theory we first need to understand how the inside of the earth is made up.

Inside the earth

The earth has a radius of 6300 km. Its centre is very hot but is kept solid by the immense pressure of the rocks above. The *core*, as this zone is called, becomes molten about 1000 km from the centre of the earth; 3000 km from the centre there is a change in composition where the core is replaced by the *mantle*. For the most part this zone is solid and it extends almost to the surface of the earth. The very thin top layer is known as the *crust*. It is about 5 km thick under the oceans and 30 km thick under the continents – very thin compared with the overall size of the earth.

---

11 a Using a scale of 1 mm for 50 km, draw a vertical column 1 cm wide on the left-hand side of your page. This represents a slice from the centre to the surface of the earth. Divide the column into the *solid core*, the *molten core*, the *mantle* and the *crust* (under the continents).

b Alongside the column, write these notes about each layer:

Crust: thicker under continents than under oceans.
Mantle: dense, dark-coloured rocks. The upper mantle is partly molten and contains slow convection currents.
Molten core: movements here cause the earth's magnetic field. Rich in iron.
Solid core: kept solid by immense pressure from above. Rich in iron.

If we look in more detail at the crust we see (Fig. 12) that the continents are made of material which is less dense than the oceanic crust, so that they are supported by the denser material below. If the continents are worn away by erosion they become lighter still and rise, but if they have to support a great weight such as an ice sheet they sink. This state of balance, known as *isostasy*, explains why much of Scotland is rising by several millimetres a

15

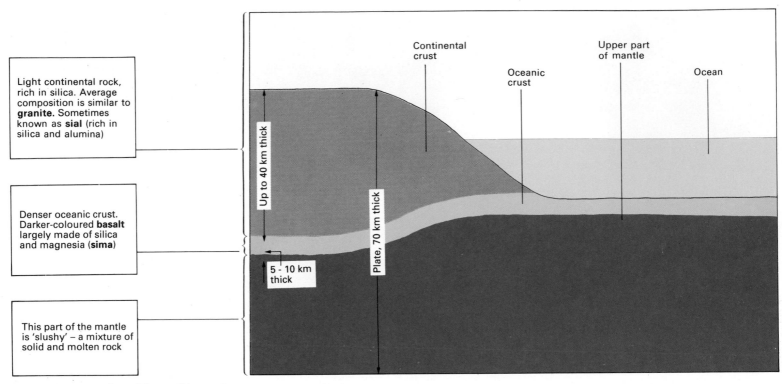

Light continental rock, rich in silica. Average composition is similar to **granite**. Sometimes known as **sial** (rich in silica and alumina)

Denser oceanic crust. Darker-coloured **basalt** largely made of silica and magnesia (**sima**)

This part of the mantle is 'slushy' – a mixture of solid and molten rock

Continental crust

Oceanic crust

Upper part of mantle

Ocean

Up to 40 km thick

Plate, 70 km thick

5 - 10 km thick

Fig. 12 Cross-section of the earth's crust

year. It is gradually recovering from the great weight of ice which forced it downwards in the Ice Age.

Looking at isostasy 🅿

Demonstrate the principle of isostasy by observing the different state of balance achieved by blocks of different densities (for example, cork, ice, and various types of wood) floating in water. Measure the proportion of each block below and above the water. Which material corresponds to continental crust and which represents oceanic crust? Note that if you place a weight on one of the blocks it tends to sink and if you take the weight off, it bobs up again.

Plates on the move

According to the theory of plate tectonics, the upper part of the earth is divided into plates (Fig. 13). These are rafts of mantle rocks and crust 70 km thick which move very slowly about the earth's surface, float-

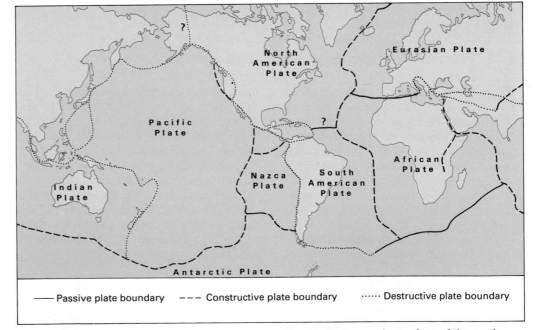

— Passive plate boundary   – – – Constructive plate boundary   ······ Destructive plate boundary

Fig. 13 Plates on the surface of the earth

ing on the slushy part of the mantle. They move only a few centimetres a year, but over millions of years this has caused continents to split apart and collide. The forces involved are immense, which

16

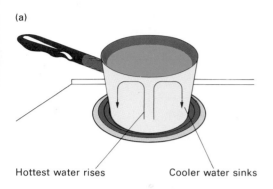

(a)

Hottest water rises   Cooler water sinks

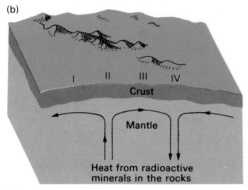

(b)

Crust

Mantle

Heat from radioactive
minerals in the rocks

Fig. 14 Convection cells in a saucepan and in the earth's mantle

explains why many of the earth's most spectacular features occur at plate boundaries.

---

12 Compare Figs 11 and 13. Name **a** five 'shields' which correspond to plates, and **b** five ranges of Alpine fold mountains which are at plate boundaries. Look up the names of the mountain ranges in an atlas.

Most geologists accept the idea of plate tectonics, though there is still uncertainty about why the plates move. One theory suggests that there are slow convection currents in the mantle, similar to those obtained if water is heated in a saucepan.

---

13 Figure 14 shows convection cells in the mantle. Where on the crust (at I, II, III, or IV) would you expect:
a the crust to split open and plates to move away from each other
b plates to be colliding?

Plate boundaries

When plates move together and collide, the plate consisting of denser, oceanic material is pushed down into the mantle where it melts and is destroyed. This is

known as a *destructive plate boundary*. Study Fig. 15 and you will see that the collision of plates produces *fold mountains* and that *ocean trenches* are formed where the oceanic plate bends downwards. As the oceanic crust slides under the continent, the rock is melted and some of it moves upwards. Huge quantities of igneous rock may solidify underground and these are called *batholiths*. Some material escapes at the surface forming *volcanoes*. Contact between the two plates also produces *earthquakes*.

In other areas of the world, plates are being created rather than destroyed, and this most commonly happens in the centre of ocean floors. At a *constructive plate boundary* the plates are moving apart. Lava wells up to 'plug the gap' and new material is added to the outward-moving plates. *Rift valleys* (see Fig. 26 on p. 21) show that the plates are pulling apart. The Mid-Atlantic Ridge and volcanic islands along it such as Tristan da Cunha and Iceland consist of new crust forming at a constructive plate boundary.

---

14 Trace outlines of South America and Africa from Fig. 17. Cut round these outlines and then place them back onto Fig. 17. Push the continents together so that they meet along the Mid-Atlantic Ridge with the letters A, B, and C matching up.

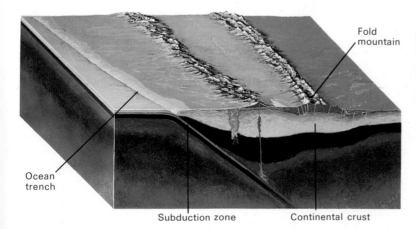

Fold
mountain

Ocean
trench

Subduction zone   Continental crust

Fig. 15 A destructive plate boundary

Transform
fault

Spreading
ridge

Fig. 16 A constructive plate boundary

In doing this you have reversed the movements of the last 150 million years. This jigsaw puzzle fit was one of the first pieces of evidence that suggested the idea of *continental drift*.

Where plates are moving alongside each other, crust is neither destroyed nor created, though molten rock sometimes finds a way to the surface between the plates. If the plates were to slide smoothly past each other, these *passive plate boundaries* would hardly be noticed, but the plates tend to grate against each other, causing earthquakes. We have seen how scientists are trying to control plate movement by lubricating the plate boundaries, making their movement smoother and more gradual.

15 a List (i) the features associated with constructive plate boundaries and (ii) the features associated with destructive plate boundaries.
b In your own words, explain how (i) Iceland and (ii) the Andes were formed.

c List five volcanoes associated with constructive plate boundaries and five associated with destructive plate boundaries. (Use Figs 11 and 13.)

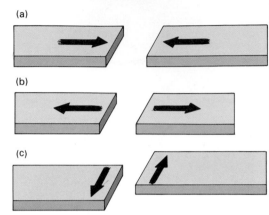

Fig. 18 Moving plates: (a) together (b) apart (c) alongside each other

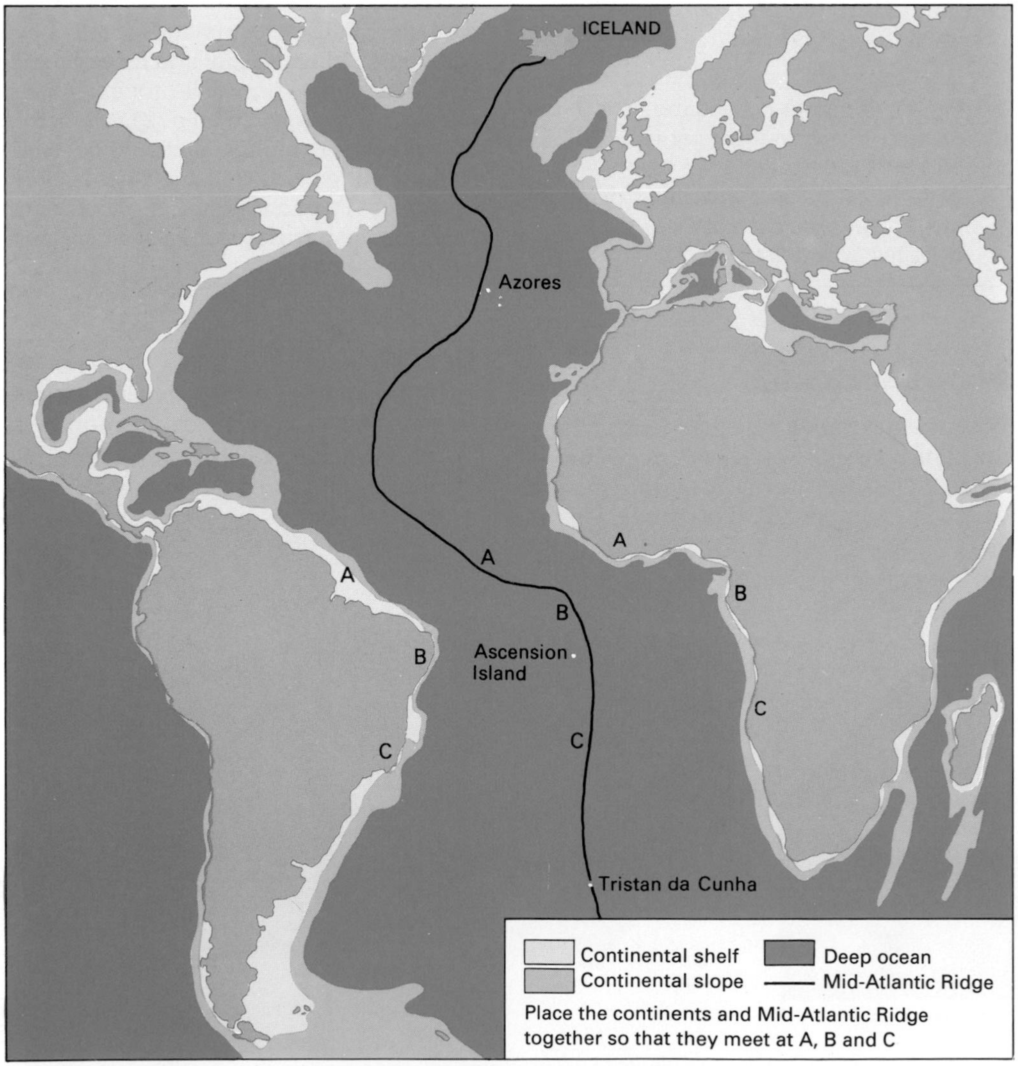

Folding

When sedimentary rocks form, their strata are usually arranged in horizontal layers (see p. 10). Yet in many places we see these strata twisted and contorted. How has this come about?

Synclines and anticlines   **P**

Hold a sheet of paper or thin card between your hands and move your hands together, allowing the paper to sag downwards. This causes a type of *fold* known as a *syncline*. Then put the paper on a table and move your hands together. The paper arches up forming an *anticline*. Match these folds with the photographs (Figs 19 and 20) and draw a cross-section of each in your exercise book.

Folds are usually formed when rock is squeezed at destructive plate boundaries. The results may be huge mountain ranges and valleys or tiny patterns in a piece of rock. The folds may be simple like those you have demonstrated with a piece of

Fig. 17 The Atlantic Ocean with surrounding continents and their continental shelves

ICELAND

Azores

A

A

A

B

B

Ascension Island

B

C

C

C

Tristan da Cunha

☐ Continental shelf   ▨ Deep ocean
▨ Continental slope   —— Mid-Atlantic Ridge

Place the continents and Mid-Atlantic Ridge together so that they meet at A, B and C

Fig. 19 An anticline

Fig. 20 An anticline (A) and a syncline (S)

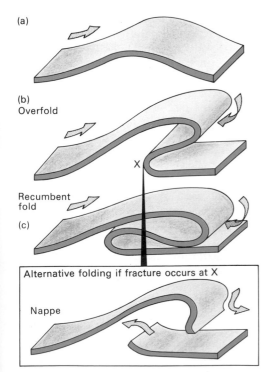

Fig. 21 Different kinds of folding: (a) simple fold (b) overfold (c) recumbent fold

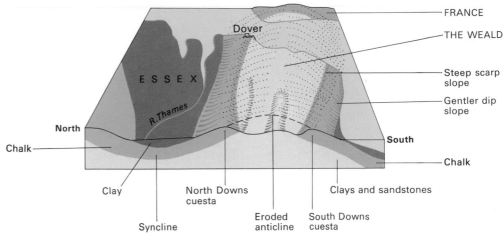

Fig. 22 Folding on a large scale in south-east England

paper, or they may be complex like those shown in Fig. 21.

Rocks in almost all parts of Britain have been folded at some stage. In south-east England the folds are generally simple anticlines and synclines, whereas in Scotland *recumbent folds* and *nappes* are more common. Where folds occur at the surface they are eroded and often difficult to recognise. Few valleys are synclines and few mountains are anticlines. *Escarpments* or *cuestas* are formed by the erosion of rocks tilted by folding, and these ridges form the usual type of hill found in south-east England (Fig. 22).

16 Write out the following paragraph, filling the gaps with words chosen from this list: *cuestas, clay, chalk, south, north, scarp, dip, anticline, syncline, Weald.*

The London Basin is a _____ which has been partly filled in with _____. The North and South Downs are the remains of a huge _____ which once covered the area known as the _____. They stand up as lop-sided ridges called _____ because they are made of resistant _____. Each ridge has a gentle _____ slope and a steeper _____ slope. The scarp slope of the North Downs faces _____ whereas the scarp slope of the South Downs faces _____.

17 Look again at Fig. 11. Notice that the youngest fold mountains in Europe are in the south while the oldest are in the north. Name two mountain ranges of Alpine age. In which countries are they? The same pattern is repeated in Britain. The Downs of south-east England are Alpine, the Pennines are Hercynian and the Scottish mountains are Caledonian. Normally you would expect the youngest fold mountains to be the highest (why?), but Britain was a long way from plate boundaries in Alpine times so only small hills were formed.

Faulting

Rocks can only be bent a certain amount before the strain is too great and they fracture along a crack or *fault*. The rocks along one side of the fault may move only a few centimetres from the rocks on the other side, though movement along major faults amounts to several kilometres.

Because faults are lines of weakness in the crust they are of great practical importance in engineering. If a dam or other large structure is built above a fault, any movement may make it collapse and many lives may be lost as a result. Faults are also studied by mining engineers. Many coal seams

19

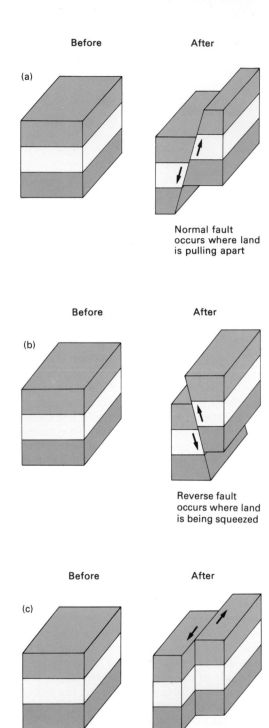

Before   **After**

(a)

Normal fault occurs where land is pulling apart

Before   **After**

(b)

Reverse fault occurs where land is being squeezed

Before   **After**

(c)

Tear fault – the movement is horizontal

Fig. 23 Different types of fault: (a) a normal fault (b) a reverse fault (c) a tear fault

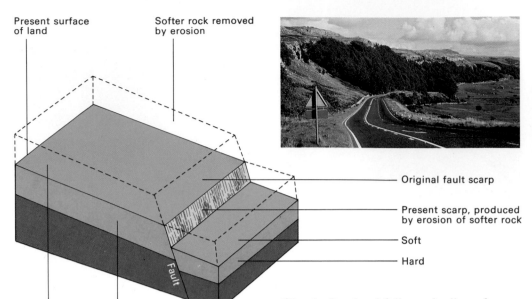

Present surface of land

Softer rock removed by erosion

Original fault scarp

Present scarp, produced by erosion of softer rock

Soft

Hard

Fault

Soft   Hard

Fig. 24 A fault scarp: Giggleswick Scar, near Settle, North Yorkshire

in Britain are expensive to work, because they are faulted. The most efficient mines have seams which continue at the same level for a good distance.

When there are large vertical movements along a fault, the land on one side may be raised several metres above the land on the other side. If such movements are frequent, the difference in height may amount to tens or hundreds of metres. The steep slope that this produces is called a *fault scarp*. Because it is so long since movement took place along British faults, fault scarps in this country have been destroyed by erosion. Yet faults still leave their mark on the landscape. Hard and soft rocks may be brought together by faulting and when the softer rock is eroded, a feature similar to a fault scarp is produced.

18 Referring to Fig. 24, describe the appearance of Giggleswick Scar and explain how it has been formed.

A fault is often surrounded by a zone of crushed rock which, being weaker, is easily picked out by agents of erosion. The Great

Glen in Scotland follows the line of a *tear fault* (Fig. 23c). This weakened the rock which was then eroded by rivers and glaciers. How much movement has taken place along the fault is not certain, but you can examine one theory in the next exercise.

19 Study the map of the Great Glen (Fig. 25). It is thought that the masses of granite at Foyers and Strontian are halves of what was once a single body of granite. Trace this map onto a piece of paper, then cut along the Great Glen fault and slide the northern part of the map back along the fault until the two masses of granite lie together. How far have you moved northern Scotland? Remember that the movement you have just reversed took place very gradually and would have been accompanied by a series of spectacular earthquakes.

When several faults occur in the same area, earth movements may raise or lower the land between them. If the land sinks between two parallel faults, a *rift valley* is formed (a rift is a crack or fault).

20 Use Fig. 26 to complete this description of the Church Stretton rift valley:

The Church Stretton rift valley is situated 20 km south of Shrewsbury in the Welsh border country. It lies between two

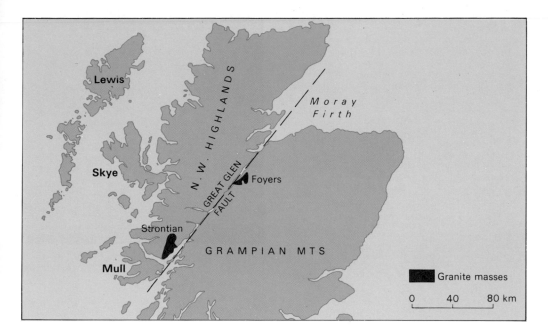

Fig. 25 The Great Glen, Scotland

21 Draw two cross-sections to explain how a rift valley is formed, showing the appearance of the land before and after faulting. Then draw two similar diagrams showing how a horst is formed.

Vulcanicity

Volcanic landforms result from the cooling of *magma*. If this happens at the surface, *volcanic* or *extrusive* rocks are formed. If it happens beneath the surface, *plutonic* or *intrusive* rocks are formed.

Volcanoes

On the island of Sicily stands Mt Etna, Europe's highest volcano, at over 3300 m. It has two *craters*, but it was not from either of these that the spectacular 1971 eruption occurred. Towards the end of March a patch of snow south of the main crater began to melt and it was here that a crack

ranges of hills, the _____ to the west and the _____ to the east. The rocks in the valley are *younger/older* than those of the surrounding hills. The valley is _____ km wide and its sides rise from _____ m above sea level to _____ m in the surrounding hills. The sides of the rift valley have been cut into (dissected) by streams such as the _____.

If the area between two faults is raised above the surrounding land, a *horst* or *block mountain* results. The Long Mynd, rising between the Church Stretton and Linley faults, is an example of a horst.

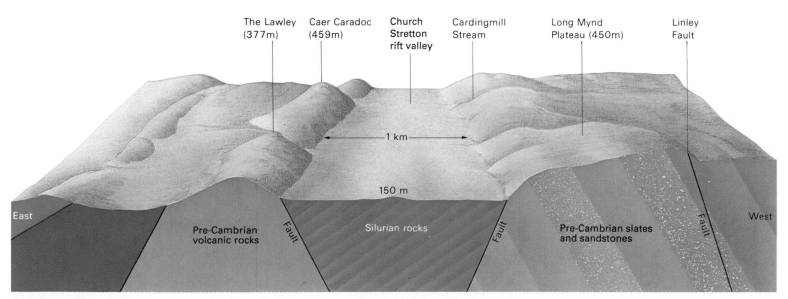

Fig. 26 The Church Stretton rift valley looking south

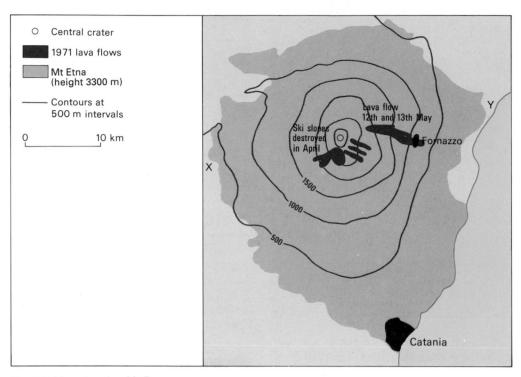

Fig. 27 Map showing Mt Etna

Legend:
- ○ Central crater
- ■ 1971 lava flows
- (shaded) Mt Etna (height 3300 m)
- — Contours at 500 m intervals

0 | 10 km

Map labels: Ski slopes destroyed in April; Lava flow 12th and 13th May; Fornazzo; X; Y; Catania; 1500; 1000; 500

Fig. 28 Mt Etna erupting

opened up on 5 April. Showers of molten *lava* were flung out, building *cinder cones* which were soon 30 m high. Lava flowed down the mountain, permanently ruining the best ski slopes, demolishing ski lifts and damaging an observatory built in the 1930s for studying volcanic activity. At night the red glow of the lava was reflected from clouds of *gas* and *steam*. On 4 May, a new *fracture* opened and yellow-hot lava was thrown out from the *vent*, building up a cone at the rate of a metre an hour. Three days later a kilometre-long fissure opened up and lava streamed out, flowing at two metres a second. On 12 May, yet another crack appeared and lava poured downhill destroying forests and vineyards, engulfing a farmhouse and forcing the evacuation of the village of Fornazzo. On 18 May, a 200 m wide crack appeared. Dark *ash* and white steam were flung into the air, forming cauliflower-shaped clouds before falling to earth and blanketing the surrounding countryside. On 9 June, gases escaping from the fissure caused an *explosion* which produced another crater.

22 List the different materials thrown out by Etna during its eruption.

23 Study Fig. 27.
  a Draw a cross-section of Etna from X to Y, using a vertical scale of 1 cm for 2000 m and a horizontal scale of 1 cm for 5 km.
  b How far from the fissure which opened on 12 May did lava run, and how many metres did it travel down the mountainside?

This eruption did an immense amount of damage, though no lives were lost. Very little can be done to control such events, though lava flows have sometimes been diverted away from villages. Volcanic eruptions are difficult to forecast, but careful measurements have revealed that the ground often swells before an eruption, and several successful predictions have been based on this. One difficulty is that volcanoes may be inactive for hundreds or thousands of years before becoming active once more, catching everyone by surprise. The division of volcanoes into those that are active, dormant, or extinct is therefore only approximate. If there has been an eruption recently and another one is likely, a volcano may be described as *active*. If it has erupted within historical times but not recently it is known as *dormant*, while if there is no record of an eruption it is known as *extinct*.

Until methods of prediction improve, we must be content with finding out more about volcanoes: why they occur, why they have different shapes, and why some eruptions are more destructive than others.

Why do volcanoes occur? Volcanoes are found where magma escapes through the crust along a line of weakness (a *fracture*) or at a single point of weakness (a *vent*). If a bottle of fizzy drink is shaken up and the stopper released, the gas in the drink forces the liquid out of the bottle, sometimes to considerable heights. Similarly, magma under the earth's surface is forced out, sometimes explosively, if it can find a way up through a fissure. This is most likely to happen in areas of folding and faulting – that is, at plate boundaries.

Britain is far away from active plate boundaries and therefore has no volcanoes, but this was not always so. The last

Fig. 29 The Edinburgh volcano: Castle Rock is a volcanic plug

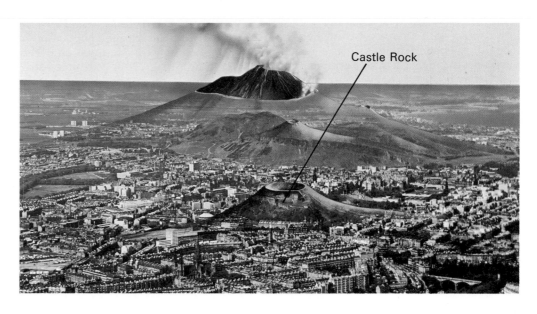

Castle Rock

volcanoes in Britain erupted 50 million years ago and have been partly destroyed by erosion, though parts of the cones can still be recognised. At Edinburgh, hard rock which blocked the vent proved much more resistant to erosion than the rest of the volcano and survives as Castle Rock, an example of a *volcanic plug*. The former cone of this volcano consisted, like Etna, of both volcanic ash and lava, though it was only about 1000 m high. These layers are preserved in the hillside of Arthur's Seat and from these it has been possible for geologists to create an impression of the original appearance of the volcano.

24 Refer back to Figs 11 and 13. There are so many volcanoes around the edge of the Pacific Ocean that this has been called the 'Pacific Ring of Fire'. With which type of plate boundary are these volcanoes associated? Name five examples of volcanoes in this Ring.

Why are some eruptions more destructive than others? This depends on how *gaseous* and how *viscous* the lava is. A comparison of Figs 30a and 30b shows that the pressure of gases in the magma chamber is an important factor in producing a powerful eruption. If the lava is viscous – thick and treacly – it does not flow easily out of the vent and tends to solidify there, forming a volcanic plug. This results in high gas pressures and explosive volcanoes. If the lava flows more smoothly, eruptions may well occur more frequently because the lava pours more easily from the vent as soon as pressure builds up, but the eruptions are likely to be less spectacular.

Eruptions vary, from geysers, fumaroles and solfataras which harm nobody, through lava flows and explosive eruptions to the destructive *nuées ardentes* ('fiery clouds').

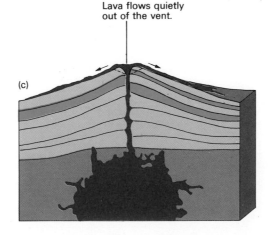

Plug of lava holds in the magma

(a)

Pressure builds up in the magma chamber

Vent is not blocked. Lava flows quietly out of the vent.

(c)

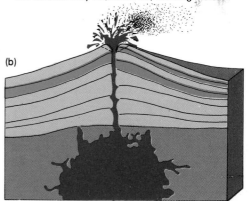

Pressure blows out the lava plug throwing ash and lava out of the vent. The top of the volcano may be blown off, forming a crater

(b)

Fig. 30 Magma is forced out of the earth like champagne out of a bottle

23

Geysers are formed when water comes into contact with hot rocks below the surface. It is converted into steam, which bursts up through a fissure, forming a jet which may be metres or even hundreds of metres high. *Fumaroles* and *solfataras* are small springs or vents giving off sulphurous gases. They are often all that remains when a volcano is approaching the end of its active life.

At the other extreme, it was a *fiery cloud* or *nuée ardente* of white hot ash and gas that rushed down from Mt Pelée at 150 km/hr to annihilate the population of St Pierre below. In two minutes on 8 May 1902, more than 30 000 people died, water in the harbour boiled, and the city was destroyed. There were only two survivors.

---

25 Consult library books and find out more about a famous eruption such as those of Mt Pelée (1902), *Krakatoa* (1883), or *Vesuvius* (AD 79).

Examples

a **Mt Pelée** (Martinique, West Indies) developed a dome within its crater before the catastrophic eruption of 1902. Later the spine shown in the photograph was forced through the dome, though it crumbled within a year. This type of volcano is often associated with destructive eruptions and fiery clouds.

Spine———

Fig. 31 Mt Pelée, Martinique, West Indies

Why do volcanoes have many different shapes?

Type of volcano	How it forms
a Acid lava dome and spine *Example: Mt Pelée*	Acid lava is viscous and does not flow easily. It soon solidifies, building up a steep cone near the vent. Sometimes the lava is so viscous that it forms a spine sticking up from the vent rather than flowing away down the sides of the volcano.
b Ash and cinder cone *Example: Paricutin*	Layers of ash and cinders, varying in size, build up a symmetrical cone with a large crater.
c Basic lava shield volcano *Example: Mauna Loa*	Basic lava flows more easily and spreads over a wide area, forming a volcano with gentle slopes. Outpourings of lava may be frequent, but are not usually accompanied by violent explosions.
d Composite cone or 'strato volcano' *Example: Mt Etna*	Eruptions are sometimes explosive, emitting ash and stones, and sometimes more gentle. The volcano, therefore, has layers of both ash and lava.
e Caldera *Example: Crater Lake*	After a major eruption the magma chamber has been largely emptied, and the volcano sinks, leaving a huge crater. Calderas (craters more than 1 km across) may also be created by violent explosions.

b **Paricutin** in Mexico started as a small crack in a cornfield on 20 February 1943. Within a week it was over 100 m high. Lava flowed from the base of the cone, which consists of cinders and solidified lava bombs sloping at 30°.

Fig. 32 Paricutin, Mexico

c **Mauna Loa** in the Hawaiian Islands is 10 000 m high, of which 4000 m are above sea level. The base of the volcano has a diameter of 400 km. During eruptions lava may flow up to 50 km down its gentle (2°–10°) slopes.

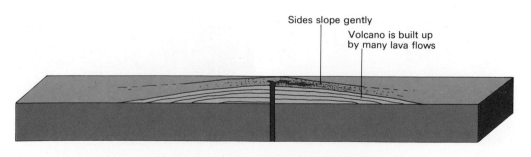

Sides slope gently

Volcano is built up by many lava flows

Fig. 33 A shield volcano, such as Mauna Loa

Fig. 34 Crater Lake and Wizard Island, Oregon, USA

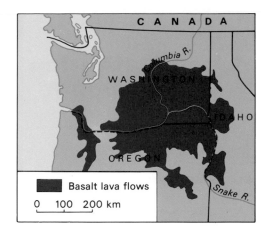

Fig. 35 The Columbia-Snake Plateau, USA

d Mt Etna has a larger proportion of lava than ash. The two types of eruption may occur at separate times or together, as they did in 1971. See Fig. 27 for the dimensions of the volcano.

e Crater Lake in Oregon, USA is roughly circular and about 9 km across. The base of the caldera is 600 m below the lake's surface, and the surrounding walls are 600 m above lake level. The caldera was formed in a series of violent eruptions about 6000 years ago.

26 Which type of lava is associated with violent explosions, and which is associated with more gentle eruptions?

27 Explain why basic lava results in wide, gently sloping volcanoes.

28 Draw a series of diagrams showing the birth of a volcano as a cinder cone, its later development into a composite cone, and its destruction when a caldera is formed.

29 From the information given about Mauna Loa, draw a cross-section using a horizontal scale of 1 cm for 20 km and a vertical scale of 1 cm for 8000 m. Compare this with your cross-section of Mt Etna (exercise 23), remembering that this was drawn with horizontal and vertical scales four times larger. Explain the differences you note.

Basalt plateaus

When runny basaltic lava is erupted through fissures rather than a single vent, it flows downhill and starts to fill up the valleys. When this is repeated time after time, valleys and then hills are covered over. The plateau this forms may spread over vast areas with little variation in height except where it has been dissected by rivers. Figure 35 shows the 130 000 km^2 covered by the Columbia-Snake Plateau in the USA, where hills 1500 m high were covered by hundreds of separate lava flows.

The Antrim Plateau of Northern Ireland was formed in the same way. It is part of a plateau whose other remains are found in the Hebrides, the Faroe Islands, Iceland and Greenland. The Giant's Causeway in Antrim (Fig. 36) clearly shows the joints which formed when the basalt cooled and shrank.

Fig. 36 The Giant's Causeway, County Antrim, Northern Ireland

3 Weathering and slopes

Weathering is the term given to the breaking down of rocks at or near the surface of the earth.

Rocks within the crust are at a higher pressure and temperature than those at the surface. As the surface of the earth is gradually eroded, the rocks become exposed to the temperatures and moisture of the atmosphere. There is also less pressure on the rock when it is exposed at the surface. As a result, rocks break up.

Rocks may be weathered in many ways but it is useful to group the processes into three types: *physical*, *chemical* and *biotic* (biological) *weathering*. Weathering is not the same as erosion, which is carried out by moving air (wind), water (rivers or the sea), or ice (glaciers).

Weathering

1 Look at the photograph on the right. Describe the surface of the gravestone. What has happened to the rock? What changes have taken place on the surface?

Physical weathering

Physical weathering is the splitting of rocks by stress and strain.

Fig. 1 Weathered rock

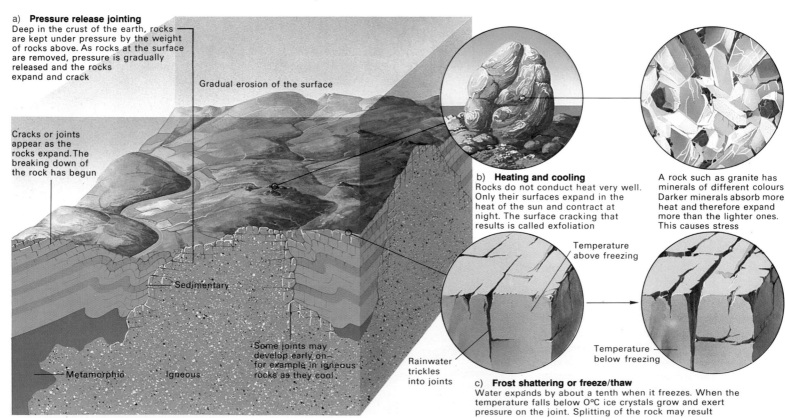

a) Pressure release jointing
Deep in the crust of the earth, rocks are kept under pressure by the weight of rocks above. As rocks at the surface are removed, pressure is gradually released and the rocks expand and crack

Gradual erosion of the surface

Cracks or joints appear as the rocks expand. The breaking down of the rock has begun

Sedimentary

Some joints may develop early on—for example in igneous rocks as they cool

Metamorphic   Igneous

b) Heating and cooling
Rocks do not conduct heat very well. Only their surfaces expand in the heat of the sun and contract at night. The surface cracking that results is called exfoliation

A rock such as granite has minerals of different colours Darker minerals absorb more heat and therefore expand more than the lighter ones. This causes stress

Temperature above freezing

Rainwater trickles into joints

Temperature below freezing

c) Frost shattering or freeze/thaw
Water expands by about a tenth when it freezes. When the temperature falls below 0°C ice crystals grow and exert pressure on the joint. Splitting of the rock may result

Fig. 2 Physical weathering

2 Study carefully the annotated diagram of physical weathering in Fig. 2.

a Write a brief paragraph on each of the types of weathering. Give each paragraph a heading.

b How might the climate of an area determine the type and extent of weathering that takes place?

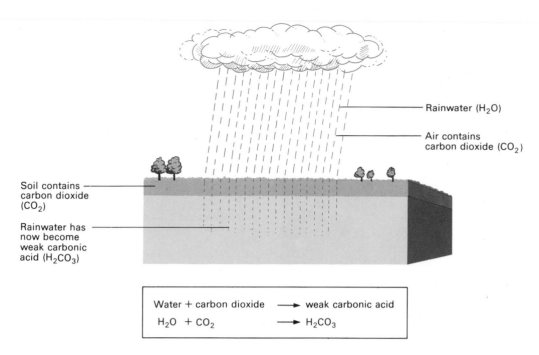

Fig. 3 Chemical weathering by rainwater

Labels: Rainwater (H_2O); Air contains carbon dioxide (CO_2); Soil contains carbon dioxide (CO_2); Rainwater has now become weak carbonic acid (H_2CO_3)

Water + carbon dioxide → weak carbonic acid
H_2O + CO_2 → H_2CO_3

Chemical weathering

Chemical weathering is the breakdown of rock as a result of chemical reactions, usually involving rainwater.

When iron is exposed to the air and moisture, it turns red. This rust shows that a chemical change has taken place. Some rocks contain iron and when exposed to the air they become 'rusty'.

There are other types of chemical weathering too. Pure rainwater can react with many of the minerals that form rocks and gradually dissolve them. Water can also cause some minerals to expand, setting up stresses within the rock in the same way as heating by the sun does.

Rainwater, however, is rarely pure. As it passes through the air it absorbs carbon dioxide and becomes a weak acid called carbonic acid. More carbon dioxide is added as the rainwater passes through the soil. This acid reacts with or dissolves some rock-forming minerals, e.g. felspar. As granite contains much felspar, it is a rock that is steadily rotted by rainwater.

Carbonic acid also breaks down calcium carbonate (of which limestone is composed) into calcium bicarbonate. This is soluble and is therefore carried away by rainwater. It is this calcium bicarbonate, dissolved in the water of limestone areas, that makes the water 'hard'. It may later be deposited as 'fur' on the inside of pipes and kettles.

This type of weathering is called *carbonation*, and its effect on limestone produces a distinctive type of scenery known as *karst scenery*. Karst scenery is described later in this chapter.

The 'natural' acid in rainfall is a major weathering process, but the effect of rainfall that is polluted by smoke and fumes from factories and cars is much more severe. When coal and oil are burned by power stations, factories, and cars, they produce two polluting chemicals: sulphur dioxide and nitrogen oxide. These form sulphuric and nitric acids in the atmosphere. *Acid rain* now affects every continent. Buildings are damaged, forests are dying, and the acid levels in the soil and lakes are rising dramatically.

Biotic weathering

This type of weathering is a mixture of physical and chemical weathering, caused by plants and animals.

3 Look at Fig. 4. Describe how this tree is breaking up the rock that it is growing out of.

When vegetation dies, it rots and forms *humus*. Water draining through a layer of humus becomes acidic and this weathers the rock below.

Another type of biotic weathering is found in coastal areas. Some animals, such as limpets, produce a type of acid which may attack rock (Fig. 5).

Fig. 5 Rocks on the beach pitted by limpets

Climate and weathering

Because so many types of weathering rely on water and on temperature changes, you will see that climate can play an important part in determining the type and rate of weathering. Many chemical reactions take place more rapidly at higher temperatures, so weathering in hot, wet tropical climates is especially effective. Chemical weathering does not take place so rapidly in desert regions because of the lack of moisture. However, the small amount of water that there is in deserts plays an important part in rock decay.

---

4 Figure 6c shows a feature known as a *tor*, on Dartmoor in south-west England. Describe the tor, noting its size and shape.

It is not known for certain how tors were formed, but it is thought they are the result of deep weathering below the surface. Some geomorphologists think this happened at a time when the climate of Britain was warmer, others believe the climate was colder than at present. Figure 6a shows how the joints of the granite are widely spaced in some parts and more closely spaced in others. The closely jointed areas

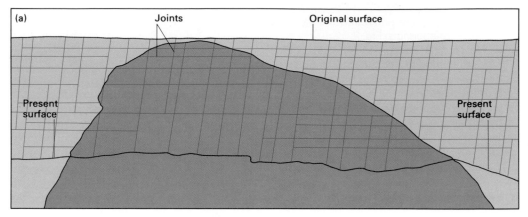

(a) Joints / Original surface / Present surface / Present surface

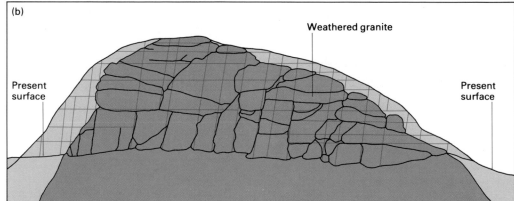

(b) Weathered granite / Present surface / Present surface

Fig. 6 (a) and (b) The formation of a tor (c) Hay Tor on Dartmoor

are weathered more deeply. The waste was removed, leaving the areas in between rounded but standing up as tors.

Weathered material

The surface layers of rock fragments help to form part of the soil, which also consists of plant and animal matter. The type of soil varies from one place to another because it has formed from different underlying rock, in areas with different climate and vegetation, on slopes of varying angles and over different periods of time. The layer of soil and rock waste (the *regolith*) on the surface is very important to the weathering process as it holds water within it, encouraging chemical weathering. Some rock, though, like limestone, has a very shallow soil as there is little of the rock left after the calcium carbonate has been dissolved and washed away.

5 Copy and complete the diagram below, adding labels to the arrows to show why the type of soil varies from one place to another.

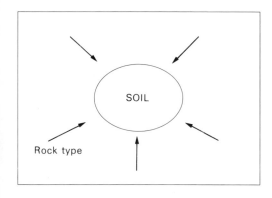

Damage caused by weathering

The processes of weathering are usually very slow. Look at the gravestone in Fig. 1 (p. 26). The stone is dated 1892. Between 1 mm and 5 mm of the surface has been weathered. A total of 1 cm has been removed from the limestone of St Paul's cathedral in the last 250 years. In London the chemical weathering has been rapid because the air is polluted by acid rain.

Buildings can also be damaged by plants. Ivy and other creepers find their way into the smallest cracks and as the plant grows, the cracks are enlarged. On ledges, grass and even small trees can sometimes be found and their roots do immense damage. Small cracks in buildings are also enlarged by freeze/thaw action.

The same type of damage affects roads. In many parts of the world there are dirt roads, made only of earth and stones. These are weathered very easily. For example, in Iceland most dirt roads have to be regularly smoothed because they are broken up by frost action. You may have noticed that when a small area of a British road is repaired, the join with the rest of the road is always sealed with tar. It is very important to seal cracks in this way, or freeze/thaw action will soon damage the road. An unsealed crack also allows plants to start growing and damage is bound to follow.

6 Examine the buildings, pavements and roads around your school. Collect evidence of different types of weathering.

Limestone

Chemical weathering is especially effective on limestone. Some types of limestone develop a number of distinctive landforms which together make up a type of landscape known as *karst scenery*.

7 Look at Fig. 7 on p. 30, which shows a map of the Ingleborough area of North Yorkshire, and Fig. 8, a photograph of Ingleborough. What do you notice about the streams in the area around Ingleborough?
a Find Ingleborough on an atlas map of the British Isles. Then make a tracing of Fig. 7. Show all the streams and rivers and the contours. Label Ingleborough, Chapel-le-Dale, and Clapham.

Your tracing shows that streams in this area begin as springs and then apparently disappear. Some of them reappear further downslope.

b Place your tracing over the geological map of Ingleborough (Fig. 9a). Trace the outline of the rock outcrops and lightly shade each one. Add a key to your tracing to show the types of rock.
c Draw a cross-section along the line X–Y, and label Ingleborough. Mark on your cross-section the points where the rock type changes, and join these points below the surface of the ground. Your cross-section should look like Fig. 9b. The rocks are almost horizontally bedded, dipping only slightly to the east. Shade your cross-section using the same colours as your map.
d On which type of rock do the streams seem to disappear? Label the cross-section with arrows to show where the streams disappear and re-appear.
e By the side of the key to your tracing, label the millstone grit and the Carboniferous limestone, saying whether they are permeable or impermeable. The 'Yoredale' series of rocks are layers of limestone, sandstone and shale. From your tracing, do you think they are permeable or impermeable?

Figure 10 shows the characteristic well-jointed and 'blocky' appearance of Carboniferous limestone. Notice how the limestone has split along the joints and bedding planes. Although there are many different types of limestone, it is mostly the Carboniferous limestone that forms the type of landscape known as karst scenery.

Carboniferous limestone is made up largely of calcium carbonate, which is easily dissolved by rainwater. There is therefore very little else left to form soil, so soils in limestone areas are thin. Figure 11 shows a *limestone pavement* where there is virtually no soil at all. The soil of this area was scraped away by the ice sheets during the Ice Age, and as soil on limestone forms so slowly, much of this area is bare rock today.

The limestone pavement is made up of large blocks separated by deep cracks. The blocks are known locally as *clints* and the cracks as *grykes*. The grykes have been formed by the chemical weathering of acid rainwater in the limestone joints. The surfaces of the clints are usually grooved.

8 a Using the photograph of the limestone pavement (Fig. 11), draw part of the pavement surface. Label the clints and grykes.
b What are the similarities and differences between this natural feature and a man-made pavement?

Carboniferous limestone is permeable. Water passes through the many joints in the rock, not through the rock itself. Figure 13 on p. 32 shows how streams flowing from an area of impermeable rock onto Carboniferous limestone may disappear down enlarged joints or *swallow holes*. These streams continue to flow underground and generally re-appear at a spring or *resurgence*. Some swallow holes are very deep. Fell Beck near Ingleborough falls 110 m into Gaping Gill – making one of the largest waterfalls in Britain (Fig. 12).

Around Gaping Gill there are a number of funnel-shaped depressions called *shakeholes* or *dolines*. You can see from Fig. 14 on p. 32 how these are formed. As the limestone is dissolved, surface material subsides and is washed into the funnel.

Some of the best-known limestone landforms occur between swallow holes and stream resurgences – underground. As running water passes through the limestone it continues to enlarge both joints and bedding planes until caves are formed. These vary in size but are often spectacular – giant caverns below the ground. These caves become enlarged by solution and by the rush of flood water through them after heavy rainfall. The shape of the underground caves and passages often depends on the pattern of joints or on their depth below the surface. Deeper passages, below the water table, are generally more rounded and tube-like. Streams in them flow at greater pressure. Passages nearer the surface usually only contain streams when the water table is very high. They are often shaped like a keyhole in cross-section, as running water only wears away the floor of the passage.

Figure 15 on p. 32 shows how limestone caves form. Water seeps through the limestone joints above the cave, carrying dissolved calcium carbonate with it. As it

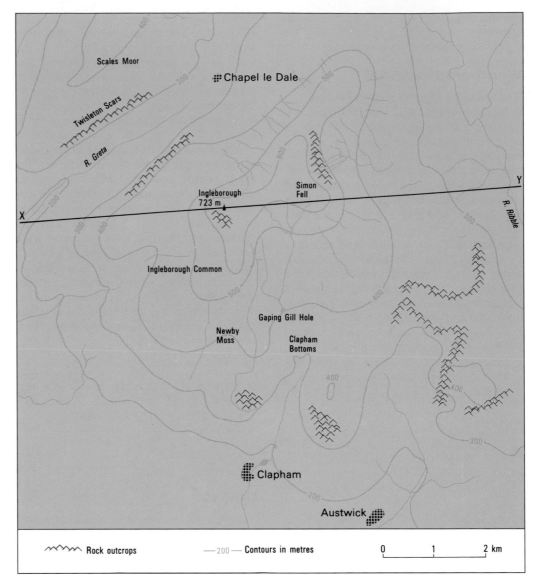

Fig. 7 The Ingleborough area, North Yorkshire

drips from the ceiling of the cave some of the carbon dioxide escapes and the water is unable to hold all the calcium carbonate. This is left on the ceiling or wall. As the drop of water falls to the floor, more calcium carbonate is deposited. These deposits are all known as *dripstone* – the best known of which are the *stalactites* and *stalagmites*.

Although much water in limestone passes through rock joints and flows underground, there may be some streams

Fig. 8 Ingleborough

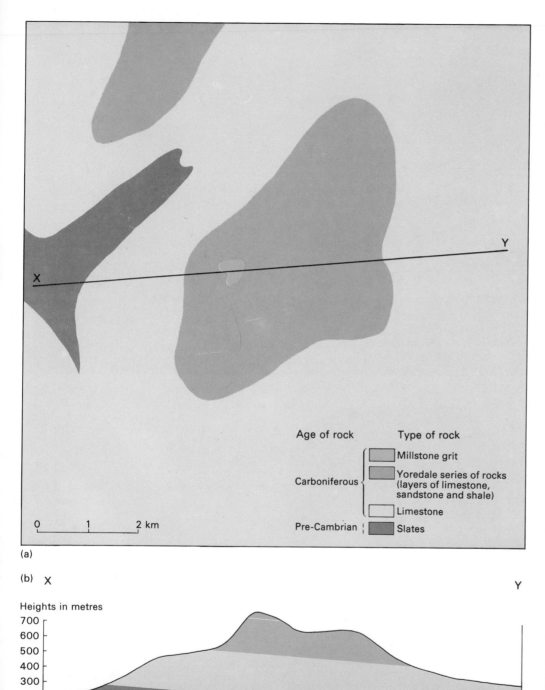

(a)

Age of rock   **Type of rock**

Carboniferous
- Millstone grit
- Yoredale series of rocks (layers of limestone, sandstone and shale)
- Limestone

Pre-Cambrian
- Slates

0   1   2 km

(b)

X   Y

Heights in metres

700
600
500
400
300
200
100
0

0   1   2   3   4   5   6   7   8 km

Fig. 9 Geology of the Ingleborough area (a) Map (b) Cross-section

Fig. 10 Horizontal bedding planes and vertical joints in a limestone cliff

Fig. 11 Limestone pavement near Horton-in-Ribblesdale, North Yorkshire

Fig. 12 Gaping Gill, near Ingleborough

31

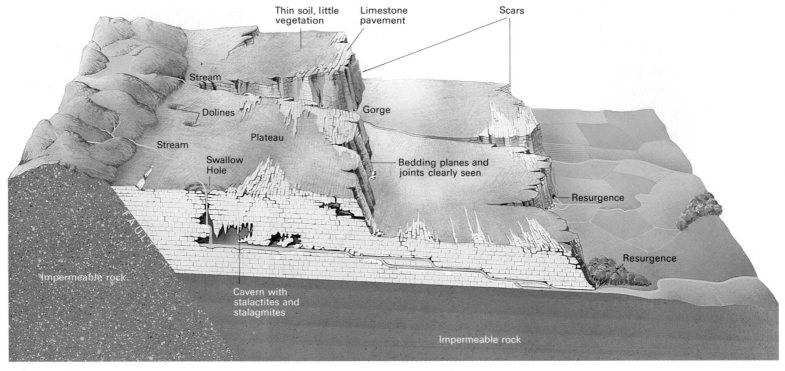

Thin soil, little vegetation

Limestone pavement

Scars

Stream

Dolines

Gorge

Stream

Plateau

Swallow Hole

Bedding planes and joints clearly seen

Resurgence

Resurgence

Impermeable rock

FAULT

Cavern with stalactites and stalagmites

Impermeable rock

Fig. 13 Karst scenery

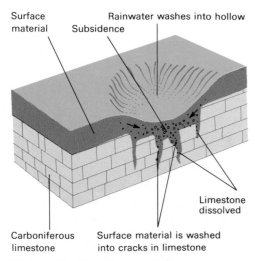

Surface material

Rainwater washes into hollow

Subsidence

Limestone dissolved

Carboniferous limestone

Surface material is washed into cracks in limestone

Fig. 14 The formation of a doline

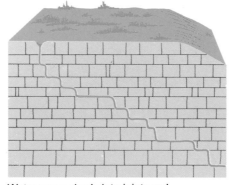

(a) **Water seeps slowly into joints and bedding planes**

(b) **Caves formed by roof collapse. Drips from ceiling**

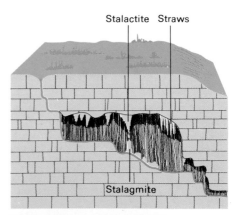

Stalactite   Straws

Stalagmite

(c) **Water continues to drip in cavern. Different types of dripstone formed.**

Fig. 15 The formation of dripstone

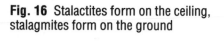

Fig. 16 Stalactites form on the ceiling, stalagmites form on the ground

Fig. 17 Gordale, near Malham, North Yorkshire

Creating a landslide

Place a brick on a board that has been covered with a thin layer of dry soil. Tilt the board and with a protractor measure the angle at which the brick begins to slide. Thoroughly wet the soil and repeat the experiment. Is there a difference between the two angles? Can you explain your result? Imagine the brick and board represent a house built on a slope. What might happen to the house after heavy rainfall? How do builders prevent this?

Landslides happen when solid rock or weathered rock fragments on slopes are not properly supported. The landslide at Vaiont occurred because the limestone slipped on the underlying layers of clay. Landslides may also occur because undercutting at the base of a slope may leave too steep a slope angle. Undercutting may be by a river or the sea, but is often caused by people. Oversteep motorway cuttings or piles of pit waste may put too much of a strain on a slope. When this happens the slope 'fails', and the material slips and settles at a new, shallower angle.

The layers of rock fragments produced by weathering move downslope by gravity. This movement is called *mass movement*. It is only rarely as disastrous as that in Italy in 1963. Most mass movement is very slow, yet it is the slowest movements that shift the greatest amount of material.

on the surface. These may occur where the flow of water is too great for the size of the joints. Some streams use their former surface bed as an overflow channel in times of heavy rainfall.

Flat-topped *plateaus* and deep *gorges* are common in limestone areas. As there are few surface streams, horizontal limestone strata tend to be worn down evenly by weathering. This helps maintain a flat plateau surface. There are limestone plateaus in the Mendip Hills in Somerset and near Ingleborough in Yorkshire. Steep-sided gorges are also common in limestone country (see Fig. 17). When rivers do flow across limestone they often cut vertically into the rock by solution, unlike the normal valley-forming processes described in Chapter 4.

Slopes

Geomorphologists are interested in how slopes change and the processes respon-

sible for their different shapes. The major process at work on hill slopes is the transportation of the layer of weathered material. This may be dissolved in the water running off the slope or may move downslope by gravity.

Landslides

9 Study the information on the Vaiont dam disaster in Fig. 18 on p. 34. Locate the area on an atlas map.
a Describe the geology of the valley.
b What caused the disaster? Reconstruct the series of events that led to the landslide.

Movements of hillsides are obviously of great importance to geomorphologists. If we can find out more about the way in which such movements take place we can take steps to predict when they will occur, to try to prevent them, and to reduce the loss of life and damage to property.

Dam Disaster Floods Piave Valley
Whole Village Submerged

(a)

Many Casualties Feared   *Bellino, Italy, Thursday*

A vast flood of water from the Vaiont Dam – the third highest concrete dam in the world – swept down the Piave valley just after midnight this morning, pouring into several counties in its path. First reports spoke of a major disaster. Communications into the area were completely wiped out. Police here, about 15 km to the south, first said that the 280 m high dam had collapsed.

Later reports said that a gigantic landslide down an adjacent mountain had plunged into the reservoir behind the dam, pushing thousands of tonnes of water over the top. Longarone, a county of more than 2000 people close to the dam, was reported by police to be completely submerged.

The civil authorities here and in Venice, about 100 km south of the dam area, reported that in the past few days thousands of tonnes of earth and rock on a mountain above the dam had been loosened by torrential rain.

(b)

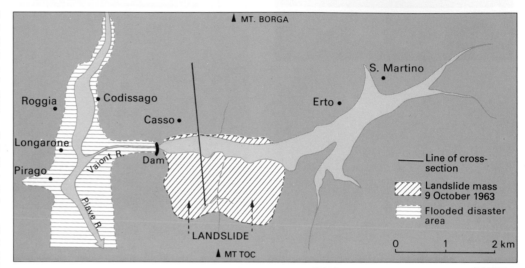

(c)

Report of an engineering geologist after the disaster

There is a long history of landslides in this area, especially on the north-facing slope of the valley. The Vaiont canyon is cut into a syncline of sedimentary rock. The rocks are composed of alternate layers of limestone, clay, and marl (a soft, limey clay). The beds dip steeply towards the floor of the valley. There was heavy rainfall in the fortnight before the disaster. The water seeped into the rocks, adding to their weight and lubricating the boundaries between the rock types. In mid-September, earth movements of about 1 cm per day were recorded. It was thought, though, that this was the movement of individual blocks of rock and not the whole mountainside moving as a mass.

On about 1st October animals grazing on the northern slopes of Mount Toc sensed danger and moved away. The mayor of Casso ordered the evacuation of the town as a small slide was anticipated. Reservoir engineers began, too late, to lower the water level. The fatal slide occurred at 10.40 pm on 9th October.

The disaster demonstrates the importance of geological conditions in dam building. Under certain conditions rock masses can weaken suddenly and movement, once begun, accelerates rapidly.

(d)

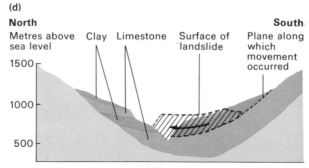

(e)

(f)

◀ **Fig. 18** The Vaiont Dam disaster (a) Extract from *The Times*, 9 October 1963 (b) The geologist's report (c) Map of the reservoir area (d) Cross-section of the reservoir (e) The dam before the disaster (f) The disaster scene Report based on G. A. Kiersch, 'Vaiont disaster', *Civil Engineering* Vol.34, 1964, pp.32–39

Soil creep

10 Look at Fig. 19. Write a surveyor's report advising against the purchase of the house shown. List the evidence for slope movement shown in the diagram.

Weathered surface material in Fig. 19 has moved downslope. The slowest type of mass movement is called *soil creep*. Figure 20 shows how this process is helped by frost. Soil creep is too slow to be observed directly. The evidence for movement in Fig. 19 has developed slowly over many years.

When soil is wet there is greater likelihood of movement. If the surface layer of soil is soaked, the layer itself may slowly flow downslope as a soggy mass. This is called *solifluction*, which means 'soil flow'. With more water and on steeper slopes the flow is faster – it is then called a *mudflow*. A small mudflow is shown in Fig. 21 on p. 36. Look at Fig. 22, which illustrates two different types of landslide – a *slide* and a *slump*. Both of these are common where strong rock overlies a weaker rock such as clay. Slides and slumps are usually fairly rapid although they may vary in size. Some slides may be of great size – the largest ever was the immense prehistoric landslide at Saidmerreh in southern Iran. A block of limestone 14 km by 5 km by 300 m slipped off the Kabir Kuh mountain, sending about 50 billion tonnes of debris rushing into the valley below.

On cliffs and steep mountains pieces of rock weathered by frost shattering fall freely as *rock fall*. The broken pieces pile up on a slope at the foot of the cliff. This slope is known as a *scree*.

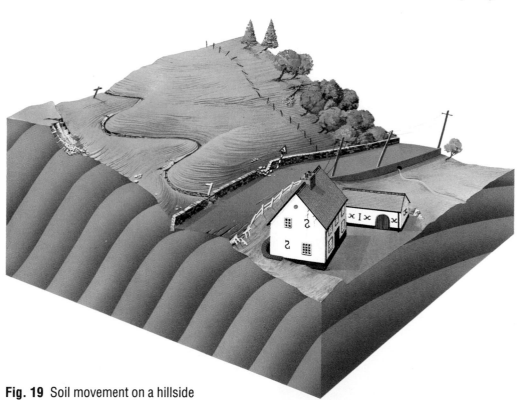

Fig. 19 Soil movement on a hillside

a) Frost pushes particle upwards

b) On melting, particle settles lower downslope

Movement of soil creep

Weathered layer of soil and rock

Bedrock

Fig. 20 Soil creep is helped by frost

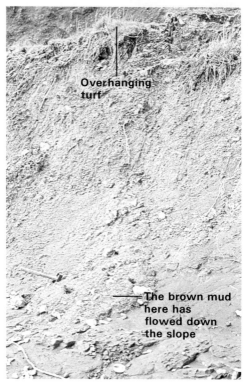

Overhanging turf

The brown mud here has flowed down the slope

Fig. 21 A small mudflow

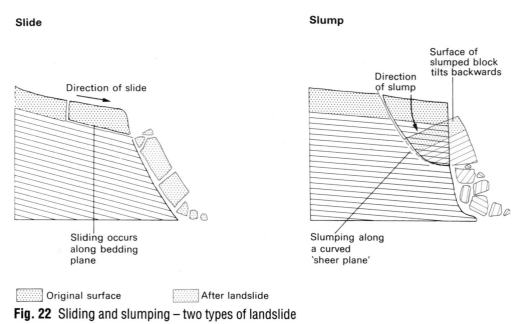

Slide

Direction of slide

Sliding occurs along bedding plane

Slump

Direction of slump

Surface of slumped block tilts backwards

Slumping along a curved 'sheer plane'

Original surface   After landslide

Fig. 22 Sliding and slumping – two types of landslide

11 Make an annotated sketch of the screes at Ennerdale in the Lake District. Label your drawing to show where frost shattering occurs.

Fig. 23 Screes at Ennerdale, Cumbria

4 | Rivers

The British landscape owes many of its distinctive features to the work of rivers. Hills and valleys generally exist because running water has cut down into the rocks. Mass movements (Chapter 3) move material down these slopes and the valley's shape may have been modified by glaciation (Chapter 5), but rivers may be seen as a basic influence on our landscape. They are also of great everyday importance to us. They provide water for our homes and for use in industry. The larger rivers are used for carrying goods by barge, and many of the smaller rivers are visited by us in our leisure time for fishing or boating. In extreme conditions of drought or floods, rivers reach the headlines of our newspapers. Historically, towns have grown up where important routes meet to cross a river at a bridging point. On the other hand, some low-lying areas have few villages or towns because of the danger of flooding.

1 On an outline map of the British Isles, mark and name the following rivers: Thames, Severn, Trent, Exe, Tees, Tyne, Tweed, Clyde, Forth, Shannon, Foyle, Dee (North Wales), Dee (Scotland).

2 Study an Ordnance Survey map of your local area. Identify any towns built at bridging points of rivers and any low-lying areas where there are few settlements.

River basins

Study Fig. 1. The marks on the hillside are *rills* – tiny streams where the water is collecting and moving downhill. They join with other rills to form streams which then meet other streams to become a river. So a river has many streams and rills flowing into it. These are known as *tributaries*.

If rain falls anywhere within the red line on Fig. 2 it will end up in the main river. This area is known as a *river basin* or *drainage basin*. The line that separates one drainage basin from another is called a *watershed* or *divide*.

Fig. 1 Rills on a hillside

3 Trace Fig. 3 on p. 38. Draw in the watersheds of the river basins draining to A, B, and C. The watershed of the river flowing to D has been drawn to show you the method. Notice how watersheds follow the hills and ridges around the valleys.

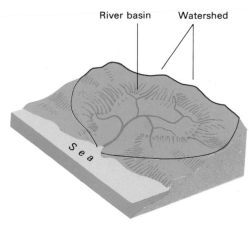

Fig. 2 A river, or drainage, basin and its watershed

4 Drainage basins may be very large or very small. Notice that each of the rivers shown in Fig. 3 has tributary streams which have their own drainage basins. Add some of these smaller basins to your copy of the map.

Making a model river basin

Make a model of the land shown in Fig. 3, using wet sand (or your school could make a more permanent model out of plaster). Make 'rain' over the model using a watering can or hosepipe with a 'rose' attached. Study the route taken by the water as it flows into the rivers. Did you draw in the watersheds correctly when answering question 3?

The water cycle

We have seen (p.7) that the water cycle is a system involving water in a liquid form (oceans, lakes, rivers, clouds, and rain), solid form (snowflakes, glaciers), and as a gas (water vapour). Sometimes the water changes rapidly from one state to another – it may evaporate from the sea to become a gas which in turn condenses to form clouds. Rain may then fall on the land to form the major input of water to the drainage basin. Water leaves the basin (output) by evaporation or by rivers flowing into the sea.

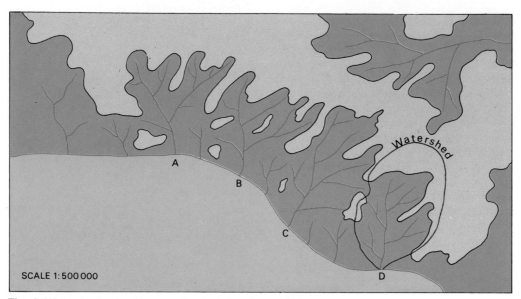

Fig. 3 Watersheds (use this map for exercise 3 on p. 37)

(use this map for exercise 3 on p. 37)

Sometimes, instead of moving rapidly through the water cycle, water remains in one part of it for a very long time. For example, it may be stored as glacier ice or be trapped deep in the ground for thousands of years. If we look at a river basin in more detail we see that there are many routes from the input (rain) to the main output (the river). Some routes are fast and others are slow. The factors involved all influence the *regime* of the river – that is, variations from day to day and from season to season.

Rainfall This may be concentrated in one season of the year, as in the monsoon of India or the winter of Mediterranean lands, giving rivers which vary greatly in size from one season to another. In Britain we do not have a seasonal drought, but we have variations from day to day which cause changes in the size of our rivers. Heavy thunderstorms in particular are likely to cause flooding.

Interception Where there is dense vegetation, some of the rainfall never reaches the ground. Water is trapped on the leaves and evaporates. Water also reaches the ground over a longer period of time, as it may still be dripping from the leaves hours after the rain has stopped. In both these ways, dense vegetation decreases the risk

of flooding, and we should bear this in mind when we replace forests with grass, arable land, roads, or houses.

Investigating interception by vegetation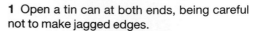

1 Construct a number of rain gauges to measure the rainfall. These may be very simple, such as a plastic funnel in a milk bottle – but they should all be of the same design.

2 Record rainfall in a gauge sited in an open area. Also put a number of gauges beneath trees and record rainfall in these.

3 Compare the rainfall recorded by the gauge at the 'open' site with the average from the gauges beneath the trees. Calculate what percentage of rainfall is lost by interception in the wooded area.

Surface runoff and infiltration When water hits the soil it may sink in (*infiltrate*) or run over the surface (*runoff*). If the rainfall is very heavy the ground may not be able to absorb it quickly enough, resulting in a large proportion of runoff. This water will reach the river quickly, causing a rapid increase in its size and a high risk of flooding. The amounts of infiltration and runoff are also influenced by the type of soil.

Investigating infiltration rates

1 Open a tin can at both ends, being careful not to make jagged edges.

2 Draw a line round the inside and outside of the can 2 cm from the bottom. Then draw a scale on the inside of the can:

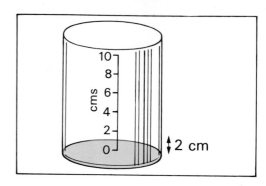

3 Select a number of contrasting sites, for example a raised flower bed, compressed soil on a playing field, sandy soil, clay soil, wet soil, dry soil. At each site, drive the tin can 2 cm into the ground.

4 Pour in water up to the mark 10 cm above the base line. Time how long it takes each centimetre of water to drain into the ground. This may vary from seconds to hours!

5 Draw up your results as a series of graphs similar to the one below.

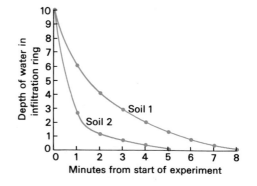

6 Explain the differences between your graphs. In a storm, which site would produce (a) most (b) least runoff? Why is the rate of infiltration often faster for the first centimetre of water than for the last one?

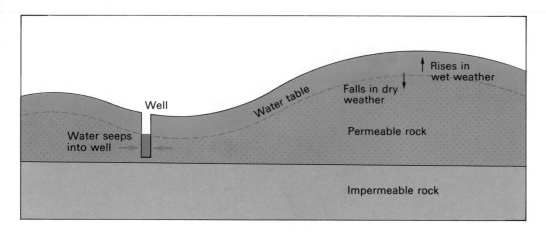

Fig. 4 The water table

River flow This is affected by all the features of the drainage basin we have been considering. If water moves quickly through the system this is likely to result in a river that experiences extremes of floods and drought. It water moves through the system more slowly, the river flow will be evened out.

Hydrographs

A hydrograph is a graph that shows how the *discharge* of a river – that is, the volume of water in it – changes over time. Figure 5 is called a *storm hydrograph* because it shows the river's discharge after a rainstorm. After the storm the river's size increases fairly rapidly. *Runoff* and *throughflow* (water moving through the soil) reach the channel during this period. After the peak (maximum) discharge has been reached the flow decreases, usually over a longer period of time than it took to increase. The discharge decreases more gradually because water is still reaching the river from the soil and from porous rocks.

6 Plot a hydrograph in the form of a bar graph, using information from Fig. 6.

The storm hydrograph shown in Fig. 7 shows that there is a delay between the peak rainfall and the peak discharge. This is called the *lag time*. The length of the lag time varies from one river basin to another and from one storm to another. Here are some of the factors that influence the shape of a storm hydrograph:

● *Is the rock permeable or impermeable?* If water sinks into the rock it takes a long time to reach the river. In impermeable areas, water flows through the soil or over the surface and reaches the river

5 Which is more likely to produce large quantities of runoff:
● steeply or gently sloping ground?
● soil which is dry or wet when the rain starts?
● soil which is loose or compact?
● soil which is permeable or impermeable?

In each case, can you say why?

Movement of water through soil and rock Many streams start as springs fed by water from underground. Water also enters rivers directly from the soil along the river banks. When water moves quickly through the soil and into a river it helps to produce flood conditions. But if it is absorbed by porous rocks it may take months to get to the river and the effect of the storm will hardly be noticed in the size of the river's flow.

Water may be stored underground depending on the arrangement of the permeable and impermeable rocks. Water will remain in a permeable layer if there is an impermeable layer beneath it. Rock strata in which water is stored are called *aquifers*. The top level of water saturation in rock is termed the *water table* although, unlike a table, it is not flat but follows the surface relief (see Fig. 4). A well is a hole deep enough to reach the water table. Water seeps in through the sides of the well until the water level is the same height as the water table. The water table may rise or fall according to, for example, the amount of rain received. In a dry spell the water table could fall below the level of the bottom of the well, in which case the well would run dry.

Evaporation and transpiration Surface runoff and moisture in the soil may never reach the river. Instead it may leave the river system, passing into the air either by *evaporation* from the ground, or by *transpiration* through the leaves of plants. This

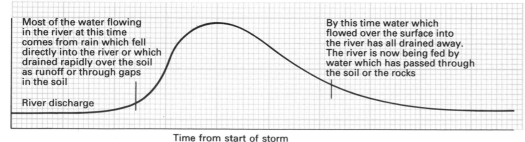

Fig. 5 How a river's discharge changes after a rainstorm

more quickly. Rivers in areas of permeable rock usually have a high *base flow* (Fig. 7) and their hydrographs are like the one for River B (Fig. 8).

- *Are slopes in the river basin gentle or steep?* Steep slopes encourage water to drain quickly into the rivers. This results in a short lag time and high peak discharge (like River A in Fig. 8).

- *Does the river basin have many or few streams?* Water moving across soil and rocks travels slowly compared with water in rivers. If rivers are close together the water can reach them in a short time and then flow quickly downstream. This results in a hydrograph similar to the one for River A.

- *What is the shape of the river basin?* The two basins in Fig. 9 are the same size but one is compact and the other is long and thin. A hydrograph measured at X will look like River A's hydrograph. This is

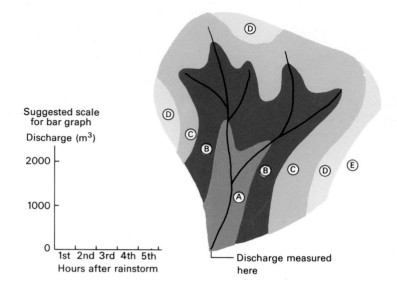

Suggested scale
for bar graph

Discharge (m³)

Fig. 6 River discharge

4.6

A steady 300 m³/hr are fed into the stream from porous rocks in the area. In addition to this, after a storm:
500 m³ arrives at the gauging station from zone A in the first hour after the storm
1500 m³ arrives at the gauging station from zone B in the second hour after the storm
1000 m³ arrives at the gauging station from zone C in the third hour after the storm
500 m³ arrives at the gauging station from zone D in the fourth hour after the storm
200 m³ arrives at the gauging station from zone E in the fifth hour after the storm.

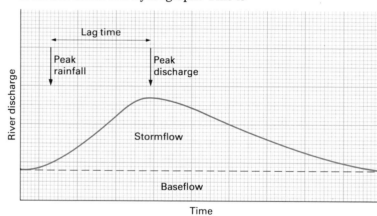

Fig. 7 A storm hydrograph

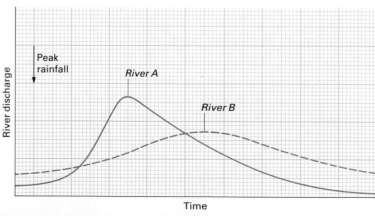

Fig. 8 Two different storm hydrographs

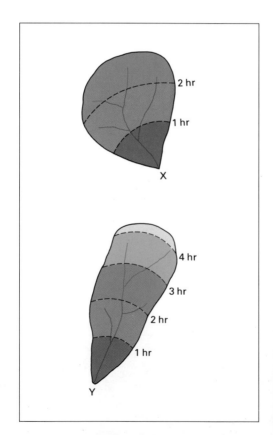

Fig. 9 Different-shaped river basins

40

because water will reach X over a shorter time period than water reaching Y in the other basin.

- *How much vegetation is there in the river basin?* In dense forests, rain is intercepted by the leaves and drips to the ground over several hours. This makes it easy for the soil to absorb the water, so there is less runoff and more infiltration. Water therefore takes longer to reach the river, which will have a hydrograph similar to the one for River B.
- *Is the rain gentle or heavy?* The soil can only absorb water at a certain rate, so heavy rainfall causes heavy runoff. After a severe rainstorm, rivers will have hydrographs similar to the one for River A.
- *Is the soil wet or dry when the rain falls?* Dry soil can absorb more rain than wet soil, so there is more infiltration and less runoff. If a rainstorm occurs when the soil is already wet, the river will have a hydrograph similar to the one for River A.

River basins combine these factors in many different ways, so flood hydrographs show a great variation.

---

7 Give two reasons why winter hydrographs of British rivers are likely to show shorter lag times and higher peak discharges than summer hydrographs.

River discharge

Recording river discharge

The flow of a river is of great importance, particularly if it suffers from drought or

Fig. 10 A river gauging station to record discharge

floods. If we want to forecast these or try to prevent them we first need to keep records of river discharge – that is, the amount of water flowing past a point on the river bank in a given length of time. *Gauging stations* which keep these records have a specially built section of channel called a *weir* through which the water passes. Where there are no gauging stations, other methods have to be used and it is quite possible to carry out such measurements with simple equipment.

Investigating the discharge of a stream   **P**

Note: *For safety's sake this exercise should not be carried out in streams over half a metre deep, or when water is fast-flowing or very cold.*

Discharge is usually measured by the number of cubic metres of water going past a given point in one second. You will see that this can be worked out by multiplying the river's cross-sectional area by its speed.

1 Select a practical place to measure stream discharge – a point where the water is neither too deep nor too fast and where there are several metres of water flowing at a fairly constant speed.

2 Measure the average speed of flow.
a Unless your school has a flow meter, the best method is to time a float over a given distance of 5 or 10 metres. This method is not as accurate, but is certainly good fun! The best sort of float to use is something easily seen and which floats well down in the water – an orange, a fishing float, or suitable piece of wood. If too much of the float stands up above the surface the wind may blow it upstream, suggesting that the river is flowing in reverse!
b Time the float over the measured distance, putting it in at several points across the river. The speed of the river is usually fastest in the middle and slowest at the sides, so a number of readings will allow you to work out the average surface flow of the river. Express your answer in metres per second.
c The surface speed is likely to be faster than the flow near the river bed. To get an average speed for the whole stream, multiply your answer for surface speed by 0.8. (A large number of experiments suggest that this is the right figure to use for most rivers.)

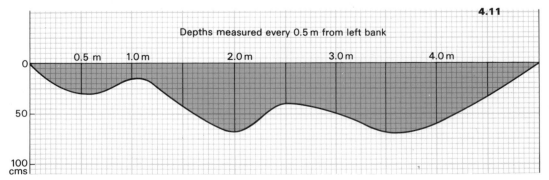

Each small square = 5 cm × 5 cm = 25 cm²
Number of squares = 810
∴ Area of stream = 810 × 25 cm² = 20 250 cm²
= 2.025 m²

Average speed of stream = 0.20 m/sec
∴ Discharge = 2.025 m² × 0.20 m/sec
= 0.405 m³/sec

Fig. 11 Measuring discharge

3 Stretch a tape across the stream. At every half-metre from one bank, measure the depth of the stream, using a ruler or measuring stick. Record these results carefully.

4 Draw a cross-section of the stream onto graph paper. Use the same scale for the width and depth of the stream. Work out the area

Measuring the discharge of a small stream – here the cross-section is being measured

represented by each square of the graph paper. Count the number of squares making up the cross-section of the stream. Calculate the area this represents in reality, expressing your answer in square metres (Fig. 11).

5 Multiply the cross-sectional area (in square metres) by the stream's speed (in metres per second) to give you the discharge (in cubic metres per second).

This practical exercise may be extended to investigate how fast the discharge of a stream increases downstream from the source, or to see how discharge varies from day to day (which may then be compared with a record of the rainfall).

Floods

Figure 12 shows the drainage basins of the River Kennet and River Mole, both tributaries of the Thames. The Mole upstream of Horley flows over impermeable clay whereas the Kennet flows across porous chalk. Because water sinks into the chalk drainage basin, this has a much lower drainage density than the clay area. The nature of the rock also influences the flow of the rivers. The Mole responds rapidly to any rain that falls. Rainfall is immediately followed by an increase in the river's size and the flow soon decreases again. This is because water reaches the river rapidly as surface runoff or through the soil and is quickly moved out of the system. In the Kennet basin there is little response by the river to individual rainstorms

Fig. 12 The drainage basins of the River Kennet and the River Mole

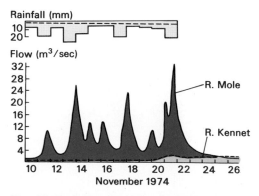

Fig. 13 Hydrographs of the River Kennet and the River Mole

The Mole Valley Floods

Heavy rainfall on 14 and 15 September 1968 caused serious flooding throughout the Mole valley. It was particularly severe in low-lying areas near the confluence with the Thames. This newspaper article describes the sequence of events.

Friday It starts on the Friday before the floods, 650 km away, over the holiday beaches of the Scilly Isles. A depression builds up, and moves first towards Biscay, then in over France.

Saturday The depression extends to southern England, and is expected to pass northwards. But instead it stays still, blocked by another weather build-up. It brings warm air and thunder, and the rains begin to fall.

Sunday It is still raining, with more than double the amount for the time of year. Roads in Surrey, and especially in the Mole valley, become impassable.

At 3 am the main A3 road is under 2 metres of water. By lunchtime the Mole has changed the Cobham landscape with floods 1 km wide. Houses are evacuated near Downside Bridge. Soon the bridge will disappear, swept away by a wall of water.

Leatherhead and the other towns along the Mole are swamped. In Esher, Molesey and Hersham, people sit in warm living-rooms watching television pictures of floods further up the Mole valley. As yet, they know nothing of what is happening even in Cobham. As they sleep during Sunday night, the rain slackens. But the damage has been done, and from now on the waters of the Mole dictate terms.

Monday Now, the combined floodwaters from the length of the Mole are starting to reach the final stage of their journey to the Thames. Around 5.45 am people in Riverside Drive, Esher, next to the Mole, wake up to hear water lapping downstairs. It is only centimetres deep, yet even as they struggle to pile furniture upstairs, the water deepens to 60 cm in an hour. The writing is on the wall for Molesey but even at lunchtime most residents still don't realise what's going on. There has been no official warning, more than a day after the Mole flooded parts of Cobham. By 4 pm West Molesey is virtually a lake. By evening the waters start to take a hold on East Molesey, and rise steadily through the night.

Tuesday The worst flooding so far, but the floods begin to recede in Cobham and Hersham. By *Friday* the Mole is back in its course.

because water sinks into the rock rather than reaching the river quickly as surface runoff. Only towards the end of the period shown is there a slow increase in the river's size. Overall the flow is far more steady than that of the Mole, and a river like this has fewer floods or droughts. It is a reliable source of water for homes and industries. The Mole is not nearly so well behaved.

Read the newspaper item in Fig. 14.

8 How many days passed between the start of the rain and the worst flooding at Molesey? Why were the floods still deepening a day after the rain stopped?

9 Did the inhabitants of riverside areas in Esher, Molesey and Hersham really need an official warning, or could they have expected flooding when they saw television pictures of conditions in Leatherhead and Cobham? (See Fig. 12 for the location of these places.)

Before the floods, large sums of money had been spent on flood control along the Mole. Sluices were built – gates across the river which can be shut to hold back the water or opened to let it through. Flood banks had been raised and changes made to the river channel. Why were these measures not successful? One reason was that the sluices were not properly operated, as the storms caught the area by surprise. Better weather forecasts might help prevent flooding. Also, the towns along the Mole Valley had been growing. Large areas of buildings and roads had been constructed. In such areas water, instead of being absorbed by soil, now runs rapidly through the drains into the rivers, increasing the chance of flooding. Finally, without spending millions of pounds it is not possible to protect low-lying areas against really freakish storms. Since 1968 further improvements have been carried out, but this still does not guarantee protection against flooding in the very worst conditions.

Fig. 14 The Mole floods, September 1968

10 You are the mayor of a town that is subject to flooding. You have obtained estimates for measures that might be taken to control this. These measures include:

- constructing dams on the headwaters of the river so that floods can be held back by sluice gates
- planting trees in the headwater area
- raising the height of the river banks
- straightening the course of the river so that water flows away more quickly.

The estimates are as follows:

Interval between floods (years)	Cost of damage done by each flood (£ million)	Cost of flood control (£ million)
20	10	8
30	35	27
50	55	50
100	100	124
1000	800	1350

You should bear in mind that:

- your council would have to raise this money from the present inhabitants of the town
- the flood which could happen every 100 years might happen tomorrow – or in a hundred years' time
- the 100-year and 1000-year floods would result in loss of life if they were allowed to happen
- when campaigning for the last election you promised to keep council spending to a minimum
- the flood control measures would have an estimated 'lifespan' of 100 years. After that, major repairs and rebuilding would be needed.

a Write your speech to the town council, saying which frequency of flood you think the council should guard against, and why you have come to that decision.
b Why do you think the consultants suggested planting trees as a way of aiding flood control?
c If the council refused to accept any of the consultant's schemes: (i) Would you encourage people to move away from of the areas prone to flooding? (ii) What sort of new land uses would you encourage in

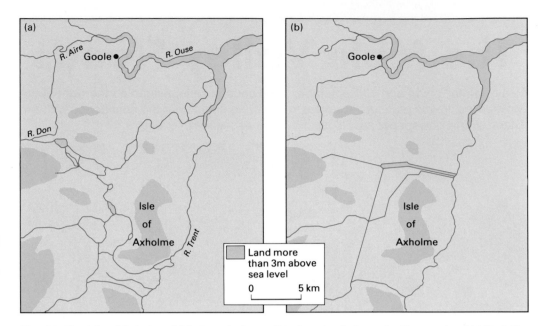

Fig. 15 The Isle of Axholme (a) before drainage (b) after the drainage by Vermuyden (1626–29)

the zone that is likely to be flooded every 20 years? Parks? Industries? Houses? Car parks? Or something else?

Artificial stream channels

The Isle of Axholme near the River Trent in eastern England is not a true island. But in the early seventeenth century it looked almost like one. It was surrounded by marshes that were frequently flooded. Rivers wandered across this low, flat land and did not take rainwater efficiently away to the sea. In the sixteenth century the great Dutch engineer Vermuyden designed a new system of channels to take water more directly to the sea via the River Ouse and River Trent. Today this is a fertile agricultural area, where drainage is carefully controlled by sluices and pumping stations.

Similar improvements have been made in other low-lying areas of England, especially the Somerset Levels and the Fens. Throughout Britain, many rivers that flow across floodplains or through towns have been controlled by dredging channels and building embankments. Deeper, straighter channels are less likely to flood and can take water more quickly to the sea.

Before engineers change natural river channels they have to think about possible side-effects:

- Straight channels usually have to be reinforced with concrete or stones. Otherwise, the river once again makes itself a naturally winding channel.
- The quick removal of water from one area can prevent flooding. But the water then arrives more rapidly at the next area downstream and may cause flooding there instead.
- Digging a new channel can easily damage vegetation and wildlife.

Figure 16 shows how new channels can be carefully designed to avoid too much damage.

11 Study Fig. 16.

a Describe three methods that are going to decrease the flood risk in this area.
b In what ways could flood protection be carried out more cheaply than in this proposal? Do you think the extra money is being well spent?

We have seen how, in the Isle of Axholme, people have deliberately set out to change the flow or the course of rivers.

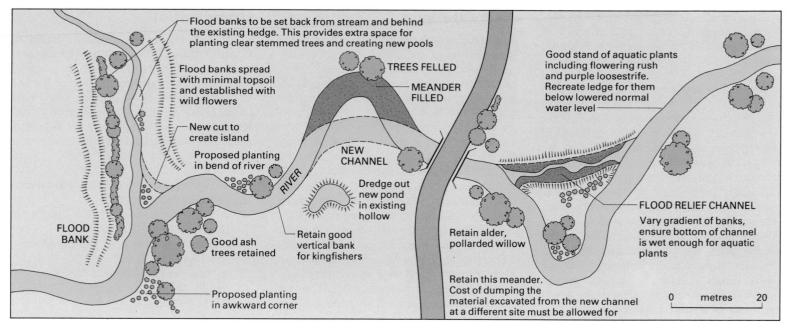

Fig. 16 Plan for a flood control project

Rivers are also changed by accident, and we look now at the effects of farming, forestry, and urbanisation (the building of towns).

Effects of farming

In prehistoric times most of Britain was woodland, but large areas of forest have since been destroyed to make fields for farming. This has affected the discharge of our rivers and has sometimes caused soil erosion. Large amounts of soil can be washed away if the land is steep or has recently been ploughed. Soil erosion is now a major problem in many developing countries where farmers clear woodland on steep hillsides. They may have to do this because there is rapid population growth and a shortage of farmland and fuel.

12 Why should rills and surface water cause more soil erosion on steep land than on gently sloping land? Why are ploughed fields more easily eroded than fields where crops are growing?

The effects of farming

Before *When the land is wooded*	**After** *When the land has been cleared for farming*
Trees intercept the rainfall. Some is lost by evaporation. The rest falls to the ground over several hours.	Most of the rain falls directly to the ground in a short period of time.
The ground can absorb most of the rain that reaches it. There is more infiltration than runoff.	The ground cannot absorb all the water that reaches it. There is more runoff than infiltration.
Because there is little runoff and the soil is protected by trees from the falling rain, there is little soil erosion.	Particularly if there is bare soil, raindrops and surface runoff cause soil erosion.
Water moves slowly through soil and rock to the rivers. Discharge increases gradually and does not reach a high peak.	Water moves rapidly into the rivers. Discharge increases rapidly and reaches a high peak. Flooding is more likely.
Amounts of erosion and deposition are moderate. Rivers carry only a small load of mud and silt.	High discharge results in increased erosion of the river channel. Material eroded from fields and from the channel is deposited where there is flooding and in the river estuary. Ports at river estuaries become blocked with silt.

Farming affects rivers in other ways too. Many farmers in areas of high rainfall and impermeable rocks drain their fields by digging ditches and burying porous pipes under the soil. These ditches and pipes drain surplus water from the soil and take it to the rivers. The extra water flowing into the rivers can cause flooding further downstream. The farmer has gained but other people may suffer as a result.

You might expect rivers flowing through farmland to be very pure and unpolluted. But many people are worried about the quality of water in rivers flowing through intensively farmed areas such as East Anglia. Large amounts of fertiliser are put on the fields and some of this is washed through the soil and eventually into the rivers. High concentrations of nitrates have been measured in some rivers which are used as a source of drinking water. Scientists are worried about possible links with stomach cancer and 'blue baby' disease.

Slurry from farms where large numbers of cattle or pigs are kept is another source of river pollution in the countryside. Nitrate fertilisers and sewage in rivers cause algae and bacteria to use up the oxygen dissolved in the water. This may have a disastrous effect on fish life.

---

13 It is easy to identify these problems but difficult to find solutions. Here are some ideas that have been suggested. Think about each suggestion and give one or more reasons why it might be objected to or be difficult to put into practice.

- Discourage the draining of marshy or wet areas by removing government subsidies to farmers for improving their land.
- Impose heavy fines on farmers who allow cattle or pig slurry to get into rivers.
- Put a tax on fertilisers so that farmers use less.
- Build more water treatment works and pay for them by taxing all farmers in the area.

Afforestation

Afforestation means planting large numbers of trees in areas that were previously unforested. We have seen the effects of cutting trees down, so we might expect afforestation to reduce soil erosion and the risk of flooding. Unfortunately, the opposite can happen in the early years of forestry. The land is usually ploughed and drained to improve conditions for the young trees. This encourages rapid runoff, which may actually increase erosion and peak discharge. Only more mature forests decrease soil erosion and flooding.

Planting trees has another important effect on the hydrological cycle. Trees transpire large amounts of moisture, so nearby rivers will have a lower discharge. This is helpful in preventing floods, but is less desirable if the rivers are used to fill up reservoirs.

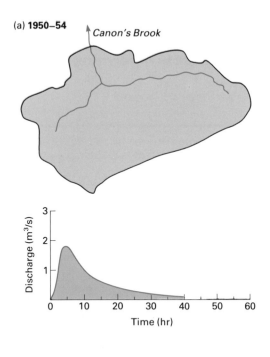

(a) **1950–54** *Canon's Brook*

Fig. 17 Canon's Brook: typical storm hydrographs for 1950–54 and 1966–68

Urbanisation

Figure 17 shows the drainage basin of Canon's Brook in Essex. In 1950 this was an area of farmland with only a small population. It then became part of the site of Harlow New Town. By the late 1960s large areas of housing had been built. Rainwater was taken to Canon's Brook by a system of concrete drains (surface-water sewers).

---

14 Study the changes between the periods 1950–54 and 1966–68.
a What happened to the length of streams and sewers in the area?
b What was the peak discharge in (i) 1950–54 (ii) 1966–68?
c How long did Canon's Brook take to rise to its peak discharge in (i) 1950–54 (ii) 1966–68?

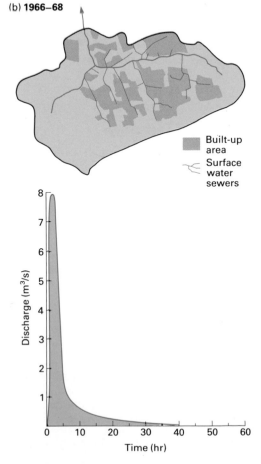

(b) **1966–68**

Built-up area
Surface water sewers

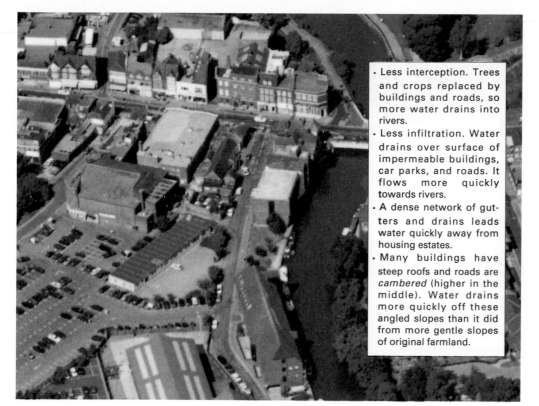

- Less interception. Trees and crops replaced by buildings and roads, so more water drains into rivers.
- Less infiltration. Water drains over surface of impermeable buildings, car parks, and roads. It flows more quickly towards rivers.
- A dense network of gutters and drains leads water quickly away from housing estates.
- Many buildings have steep roofs and roads are *cambered* (higher in the middle). Water drains more quickly off these angled slopes than it did from more gentle slopes of original farmland.

Fig. 18 The effects of urbanisation on river discharge

The main effects of urbanisation were the shorter lag time and higher peak discharge. Figure 18 shows some of the reasons for these changes. The larger peak flows of rivers coming from urban areas can cause flooding and erosion further downstream. The water is also likely to be polluted, even if there is careful control of factory effluent and sewage. During dry spells roads get a covering of dirt and oil. The rain washes this into drains and it flows into the rivers. In the first few hours after a rainstorm, rivers contain large amounts of this pollution, which can damage fish life downstream.

River valleys

A river's energy

In everyday life we use our energy for lifting things, or for walking and running. The energy comes from the food we eat.

An athlete who uses a great deal of energy often has to eat more to get this energy. A river is in some ways similar. It uses energy to erode its bed and banks and to transport its load of pebbles and fine material. If it is to carry out a great deal of this work it needs a lot of energy. A river's energy depends on the slope of the land and the amount of water flowing along it, so we can say that the steeper the gradient and the larger the river, the more energy it has.

What is this energy used for? Most of it (95%) is used simply to keep the river flowing. As water moves over the bed and banks, these tend to slow it down, a process known as *friction*. In a small channel or a channel with very rough bed and banks, friction slows the river even more. A river at low water has less energy than the same river at high water, simply because it is smaller. In addition the low-water river has to use more of its energy in overcoming friction. As a result, the high-water river flows much faster, erodes its

channel, and transports more material downstream.

You might expect a river in its upper course, where the gradient is generally steep, to flow faster than a river further downstream, but this is not the case. The upland river has a small, rough channel and uses up more of its energy in overcoming friction, whereas less of the water in a lowland river is slowed down by the bed and banks. The result is that the average speed of a mountain torrent is very similar to that of a large river flowing over a lowland. It is true that in places such as waterfalls and rapids the upland stream may have sections of very fast flow, but this is balanced out by eddies where water may move downstream very slowly, so the average speed is not as fast as one might imagine.

The fastest part of the river is well away from the bed and banks

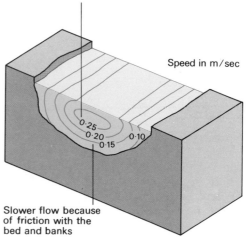

Speed in m/sec

Slower flow because of friction with the bed and banks

Fig. 19 The speed of water varies within a river

The 5% or so of energy left over after a river has overcome friction may be used to wear away or *erode* material from the edge of the channel and to *transport* (carry) it downstream. If the river is transporting material and there is a decrease in its energy, the material may be *deposited* (dropped to the river bed).

There is a balance between the energy a stream has and the work it carries out. The shape of the channel is a result of the balance that has been achieved. The delicacy of this balance is sometimes forgotten and can easily be upset by human action. When a dam is built across a river, deposition occurs in the lake behind the dam. The lake is gradually filled in. The river downstream of the dam is starved of sediment and may erode its channel vigorously.

15 A fast-flowing river is likely to have more energy for erosion than a slow one. Bearing this in mind, is it *erosion* or *deposition* that is more likely when
a a river flows from a steep to a gentle gradient
b heavy rainfall causes the river to increase in size
c a river speeds up because the channel is smoother and larger
d a lot of material falls into the river when a section of bank collapses?
Give reasons for each of your answers.

Fig. 20 Potholes in a river bed – the hammer is about 30 cm long

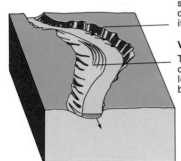

Lateral erosion
The river erodes sideways, cutting into its banks

Vertical erosion
The river erodes downwards, lowering its bed

Fig. 21 Vertical and lateral erosion in a river

Erosion

Processes of erosion Moving water erodes best when it is carrying particles which it throws against the bed and bank. These in turn dislodge more particles, a process known as *abrasion* or *corrasion*. This process can form *potholes* in the river bed. A hollow in the stream bed is deepened by stones whirled round and round by the force of the water.

16 Study Fig. 20. Describe these potholes in the river bed, mentioning their shape and estimating their depth and width. By itself, water can only erode soft material unless it is travelling very fast. This process is known as *hydraulic action*.

17 Use a dictionary to find out the meaning of the word 'hydraulic'. What other words start with 'hydra' or 'hydro'?

A river may also dissolve its bed and banks. Rivers flowing over chalk or limestone carry out much of their erosion in this way (*solution*).

As the load of a river is carried downstream, particles knock against each other and also hit the bed and banks. In doing so, they erode each other, becoming smaller and more rounded. In this process, known as *attrition*, material is gradually worn down to form fine rock particles called *silt*.

Results of erosion Erosion may be mainly *vertical* or *lateral* (horizontal). In upland areas most erosion takes place vertically on the bed of the river, as shown by the presence of potholes, or of *waterfalls*. Waterfalls or *rapids* may form where a stream plunges into a deep valley formed by a glacier in the Ice Age, where it crosses a fault line, or where it flows from hard to soft rock.

18 Find out the names and heights of some of the world's largest waterfalls.

Investigating the formation of a waterfall **P**

Make a slope of damp sand in a plastic tray, as shown opposite (Fig. 22). The layer of plasticine represents a layer of hard rock. Make a stream channel down the slope and pour water gently into the head of the channel. Observe the formation of a waterfall and sketch the features associated with it, comparing them with Fig. 23.

Erosion in uplands forms valleys which are narrow and steep sided. If downward erosion is very rapid or the valley sides are very hard, a gorge with almost vertical sides may result. More often the sides slope down to the river like a letter V, which is why many upland valleys are described as *V-shaped*.

Fig. 22 A model waterfall

Water from tap
or watering can

Plastic tray

Drain hole

Bucket

Block under
end of plastic
tray to produce
a slope

Layer of
plasticine
reaches the
surface here

Damp sand, with
valley in centre

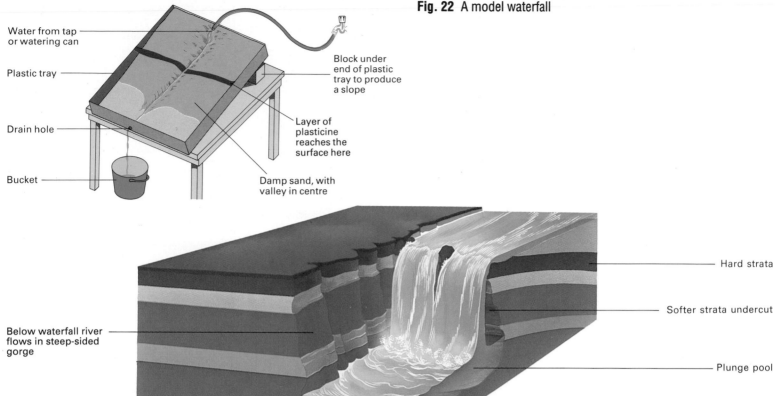

Hard strata

Softer strata undercut

Below waterfall river
flows in steep-sided
gorge

Plunge pool

Fig. 23 The features of a waterfall

Fig. 24 Interlocking spurs in a river valley

The effect of vertical erosion is also seen in upland areas where a river is swinging from side to side. It cuts down into the land, producing *interlocking spurs* (Fig. 24).

19 Figure 25 on p. 50 shows an upland stream which has cut into the surrounding hills.
  a Calculate the gradient of the stream.
  b Draw a cross-section of the valley from A to B. Would you describe this as a gorge or a V-shaped valley?
  c Do you think you would be able to see straight up the valley, or would the view be blocked by interlocking spurs?

In lowland areas where the river is nearer to sea level, it cannot erode downwards very much. Vertical erosion is slower and the effects of lateral erosion are more easily seen. Most lateral erosion takes place where a river is swinging from side to side or *meandering*.

20 Draw a sketch map of the river shown in Fig. 26 on p. 50. Your map should show the shape of the river as it would appear if you were looking straight down at it from above. Mark the *river cliff* and shade the area of recently deposited material which has no grass growing on it. What evidence is there on the photograph that part of the river cliff has collapsed into the river fairly recently?

21 Trace Fig. 27 on p. 50, which shows where the fastest-flowing current is found along a meandering river. Why do you think the current sometimes hits the banks of the river rather than staying in the middle of the channel? Mark on your tracing the places where you would expect to find erosion and deposition.

Investigating the behaviour of a meandering river **P**

Set up a miniature stream as in the last practical exercise, but make the sand slope more gently, leave out the plasticine layer, and give the stream a meandering course. Observe the movement of sand particles in the stream channel. Are there particular places where erosion or deposition occurs? Are river cliffs formed? If not, experiment with the shape of the meanders, the gradient of the stream, and the amount of water you are pouring down the channel.

22 The extent to which a river meanders depends mostly upon its size. The larger the river, the bigger its meanders. The extent to which a river meanders can be described by a simple *sinuosity ratio*:

$$\frac{\text{River length AB}}{\text{Straight line distance AB}} \times 100$$

With this measure, a straight river has a sinuosity ratio of 100. The larger the meanders, the bigger this figure becomes.

a Work out the sinuosity ratio between A and B on Fig. 29.

b Use an Ordnance Survey map or series of maps to follow a river from its source to the sea. Measure the sinuosity ratio near the source, near the middle of the river, and near the mouth. Is it true that the meanders get bigger as you go downstream? Does the sinuosity ratio gradually increase?

The formation of river cliffs by erosion on the outer, downstream side of a meander (Fig. 26) shows that the position of a meander is gradually changing. Over very long periods of time the meanders will bite into the interlocking spurs further and further until they erode them altogether (Fig. 28). You can demonstrate in a few seconds what a river achieves in a thousand years by lying a length of rope on the ground and flicking one end from side to side. A pattern of waves passes along the rope. Think of these as the meanders

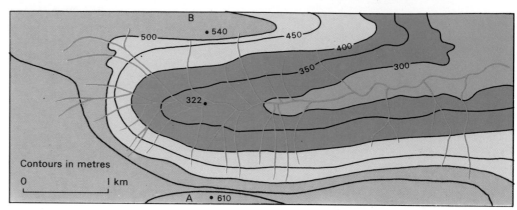

Fig. 25 Map of an upland stream: Snaizeholme Beck, West Yorkshire

Fig. 26 Lateral erosion in a meandering stream

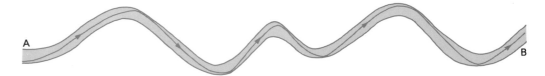

Fig. 27 Where the current flows fastest in a meandering river

changing their course and moving downstream. The area covered by the waves which pass along the rope is similar to the *floodplain* of a river, the wide flat valley floor cut by the meanders as they move down valley. The spurs are cut back to form more or less parallel *bluffs* and the river is no longer flowing in a narrow V-shaped valley.

A close examination of the floodplains of many rivers will produce evidence for the changing patterns of meandering over

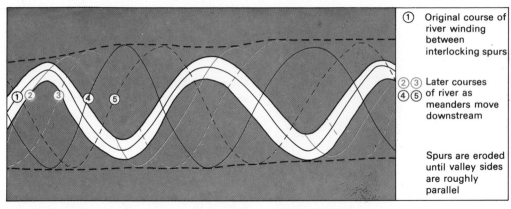

① Original course of river winding between interlocking spurs

②③④⑤ Later courses of river as meanders move downstream

Spurs are eroded until valley sides are roughly parallel

Fig. 28 Interlocking spurs are eventually removed by river meanders

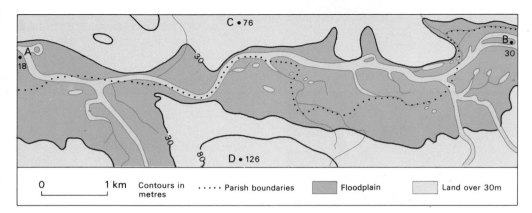

C • 76

A 18

B • 30

30

30

80

D • 126

| 0 | 1 km | Contours in metres | · · · · Parish boundaries | Floodplain | Land over 30m |

Fig. 29 The valley of the River Lune, Lancashire

the years. Figure 29 shows the valley of the River Lune in Lancashire. Parish boundaries, drawn up about a thousand years ago, would have followed the course of the river. In some places they still do, but elsewhere the river has changed its course. Also notice the streams and lakes on the floodplain. Many of these are the remains of former meanders, now bypassed by the river. Their formation is explained in Fig. 30.

In some valleys, *terraces* – abandoned sections of floodplain slightly above river level – are another form of evidence that meanders have changed their course. The river has cut down slightly but has moved a great deal horizontally. Its former routes across the floodplain are shown by the shape of the terraces (see Fig. 31 on p. 52).

23 a Calculate the gradient of the River Lune from A to B on Fig. 29.

b Draw a cross-section of the valley from C to D. Mark the present position of the river and label the floodplain and the bluffs.

c Would you be able to see straight up the valley, or would the view be blocked by interlocking spurs?

d Calculate the sinuosity ratio of the River Lune between A and B.

Transport

Rivers transport their load in several ways, and these can easily be demonstrated using a piece of guttering.

4.30

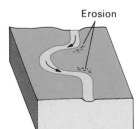

Erosion

(a) River is meandering. Erosion on the outside of bends leads to the formation of ...

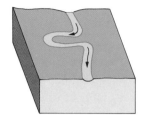

(b) ...'swan's neck' meander.

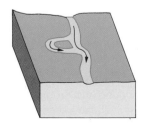

(c) In time of flood, water takes a 'short cut' across the neck of the meander. If this becomes the main channel ...

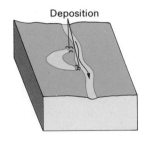

Deposition

(d) ...the older channel may be abandoned, becoming an ox-bow lake when deposition occurs alongside the new channel.

Fig. 30 The formation of ox-bow lakes

Fig. 31 River terraces, Swaledale, near Keld, North Yorkshire

Investigating the movement of material in a miniature river 🅿

1 Allow water to flow along the gutter. It may appear to be carrying no load but this is not the case. Minerals are dissolved in the water, particularly in areas of chalk or limestone. This is known as *solution load*. Water containing large amounts of chalk or limestone in solution is known as *hard water*. Soap does not lather as easily in hard water as it does in soft water. The 'fur' that sometimes forms in kettles is another sign that the water is hard (see p. 27).

2 Drop fine particles of dried and ground-up clay soil into your 'stream'. These will not sink straight to the bottom, because the flow of water is turbulent (see Fig. 33). Material carried along in this way is known as *suspension load*. Some rivers are given a distinct colouring by their suspension load – for example the black of the River Negro (a tributary of the Amazon), or the pale colour of the White Nile.

3 You may observe some of the larger particles hitting the bottom and then bouncing back up into the stream. Transport in this way, as a series of hops, is known as *saltation*.

4 Drop sand particles into the stream. These will be rolled along the bottom as *traction load* or *bed load*.

Fig. 32 Model of a river transporting its load

Similar experiments could be carried out in a real stream and could then be taken a step further, as suggested below.

Investigating the influence of the speed of a stream on the size of the load that may be transported 🅿

1 Measure the speed of a stream at several points, to get a range from fast to slow.
Note: *Remember to take care if you are investigating a fast-flowing section of water.*

2 Make up several sets of particles, from fine clay through sand and small pebbles to large pebbles.

3 Starting with the first material, at each point see which material is moved by the stream and which is not.

4 Work out the speed of flow needed to move each type of material.

Rivers erode material from their bed or banks and are supplied with soil or boulders by mass movements on the valley sides. Provided the river has enough energy, this debris is carried away downstream. But for much of the year little material is eroded or transported because the speed and discharge of the river are too small. Occasionally though, when the river completely fills its channel, it can carry huge quantities of material. Figure 34 shows a stream descending to Loch Maree

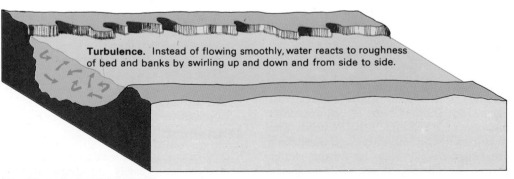

Turbulence. Instead of flowing smoothly, water reacts to roughness of bed and banks by swirling up and down and from side to side.

Fig. 33 Turbulent flow in a river

Fig. 34 Coarse bed load

in north-west Scotland. The large quartzite boulders littering its bed were brought down from the mountains in March 1968 when 16.5 cm of rain fell in 24 hours. Since then they have hardly moved.

---

24 Draw the axes of a graph like the one below, and plot the following figures:

River discharge (cubic metres per second)	Sediment carried (grammes per second)
0	0
1	10
2	60
3	150
4	300
5	580

Would you say that a small increase in discharge makes a small or a big difference to the amount of material a river carries?

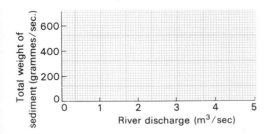

Fig. 35 Graph to show river discharge and sediment carried

Deposition

We have seen how material may be dropped where a river loses the energy to transport all of its load. We look here at four examples of how this may occur.

Point bars Look back to Fig. 26 on p. 50. When a river flows around a meander it erodes material on the outside of the bend but deposits some of its load in the slower-moving water on the inside of the bend, forming a *point bar* (Fig. 36).

Material on floodplains If a river bursts its bank it may spread out over a wide floodplain. When this happens there are large areas of silt-laden water moving very slowly over the gently sloping land. Coarse material tends to be deposited soon after leaving the river channel and this may build up to form *levées* along the banks of the river (Fig. 37). Where would settlements usually be built in an area like this? People have often added to the levées in an effort to build high banks which will prevent flooding.

Further from the river, the fine suspended load sinks to the bottom and is left as a thin deposit of mud. Over the centuries most floodplains have built up a considerable thickness of silt (*alluvium*) in this way. These areas often form fertile land for agriculture, though it may be used for pasture rather than being ploughed up if it is very damp or frequently flooded.

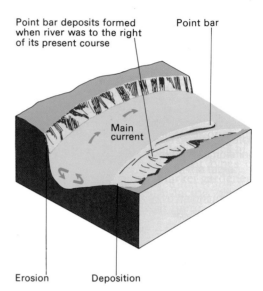

Fig. 36 Formation of a point bar

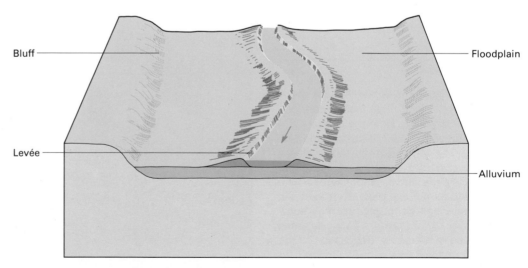

Fig. 37 Levées – note the danger of flooding if the banks burst

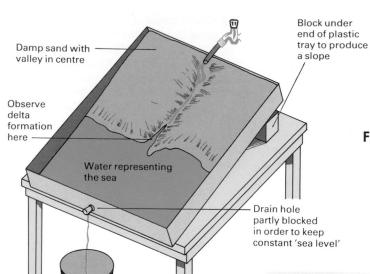

Damp sand with valley in centre

Observe delta formation here

Water representing the sea

Block under end of plastic tray to produce a slope

Drain hole partly blocked in order to keep constant 'sea level'

Fig. 38 Modelling a delta

There are no large deltas around the British coast. Instead, much of the deposition has taken place in estuaries. In the Thames estuary, for example, large areas of mud flats are exposed at low tide, and these consist of material deposited by the river.

Alluvial fans Where a stream flowing steeply through mountains and carrying a big load reaches a lowland it is likely to drop much of its load. Over the years this material can build up in a fan shape, rather like a steeply sloping delta at the edge of the lowlands rather than at the edge of the sea.

Deltas

Investigate the growth of a delta P

Arrange a plastic tray containing sand as shown above. Observe the mouth of the river as you allow water to flow down the channel. Sand is deposited in the water that represents a lake or the sea. Why do you think this happens? The new area of land formed in this way is called a *delta*. Keep a record of its growth, noting changes in its shape and in the pattern of the stream channel.

---

25 Use an atlas to make sketch maps of the Mississippi delta, Nile delta, and one other major delta. Note the difference in shape between the Mississippi and Nile deltas. The Mississippi delta is called a *bird's-foot delta* because of its shape. The Nile delta with its smoother coastline is called an *arcuate delta*. Note how the river entering a delta splits up into a number of *distributaries*. This happens because material is deposited in the actual channel of the river, forcing it to split.

Fig. 39 An alluvial fan

Case Study

The River Loughor

The River Loughor (Figs 40 and 41) flows into the sea near Llanelli in South Wales. The photographs in Fig. 41 on p. 56 are arranged in order from the river's source to its mouth.

26 *The river's long-profile* Draw a long-profile of the river – that is, a diagram showing the slope from its source to its mouth. Use a vertical scale of 1 cm for 50 m and a horizontal scale of 1 cm for 1 km.

Distance from source (km)	Height above sea level (m)
0	230
0.5	190
1	183
2	160
3	137
4	120
5	96
6	60
7	40
8	33
12	14
20	1

A more detailed diagram would show that the upper part of the river's course is not only steeper but also more irregular than the lower part. Refer to Fig. 41a on p. 56, and describe the bed of the river in its upper course.

27 *The valley cross-profile* Study the three cross-profiles of the Loughor valley (Fig. 40). Describe how the valley's cross-profile changes from source to mouth. Explain the changes you observe.

28 *The course of the river in plan* – that is, as seen from above
a Use the enlargements of part of the lower course and part of the upper course in Fig. 40 to work out a sinuosity ratio for each length of the river.
b Draw a sketch map or series of sketch maps showing how you think meander A (Fig. 41c) may change its shape during the next 5000 years.

Fig. 40 The valley of the River Loughor

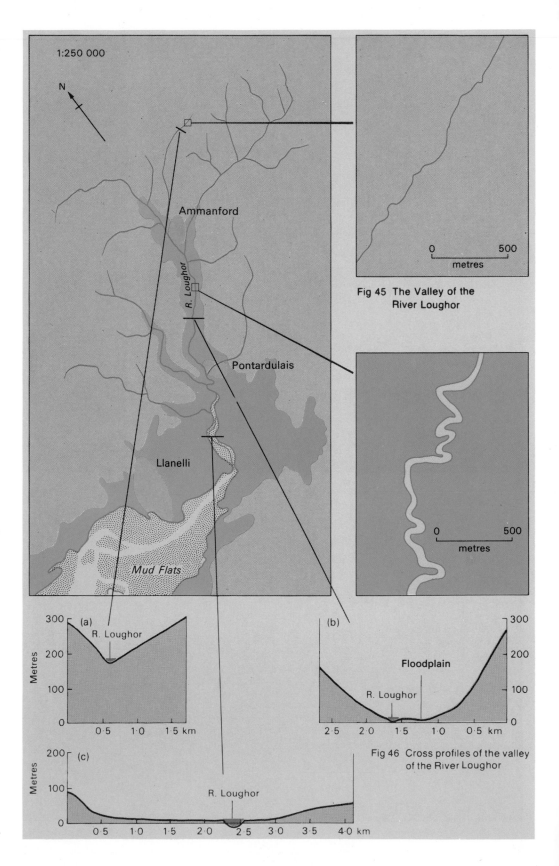

Fig 45 The Valley of the River Loughor

Fig 46 Cross profiles of the valley of the River Loughor

(a)

(b)

(c)

Fig. 41 The River Loughor valley

5 | Ice

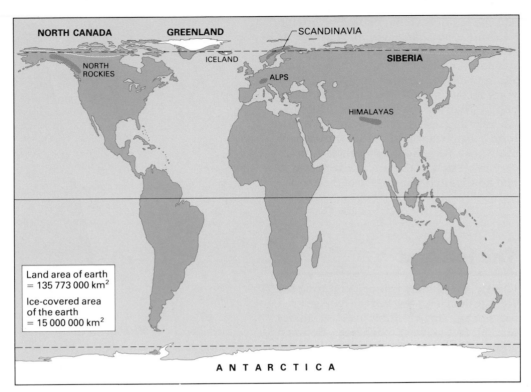

Look at Fig. 1. This photograph shows part of the Vatnajökull, an ice-covered mountain in Iceland. At the present time, large areas of the earth's surface are covered with ice.

Land area of earth
= 135 773 000 km²

Ice-covered area
of the earth
= 15 000 000 km²

Fig. 1 Part of the Vatnajökull ice cap, Iceland

1 Refer to Figs 1 and 2.
a Briefly describe the surface of the Vatnajökull ice cap.
b Work out the percentage of the earth's land area that is covered by ice today:

% land covered by ice =
$$\frac{\text{area covered by ice}}{\text{total area of land}} \times 100$$

c The surface areas of the earth that are more or less permanently covered by ice may be grouped into two types of location. What are they?

During the Ice Age, 30% of the surface of the earth was covered by ice – far more than today. Ice covered much of Britain

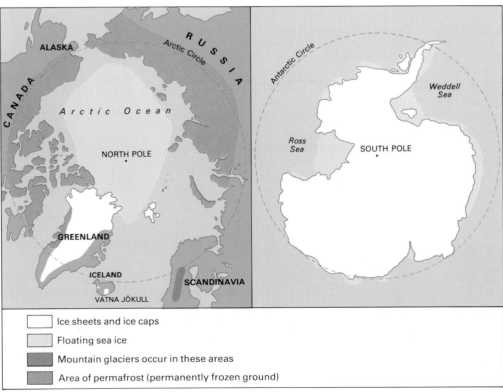

Ice sheets and ice caps

Floating sea ice

Mountain glaciers occur in these areas

Area of permafrost (permanently frozen ground)

Fig. 2 Ice on the surface of the earth

and the landforms that existed before the ice came were changed both by the ice itself and by its meltwater. Ice began to spread over Britain about 2 million years ago and disappeared only about 10 000 years ago, a time known as the Pleistocene period. Many of the landforms the ice has left may be clearly seen today, and they form a significant part of the landscape of the British Isles. So geomorphologists are very interested in the way the ice behaves and how it alters the surface of the earth.

The Ice Age

Clearly, the climate was colder during the Ice Age than it is now, but the Ice Age itself was not one single, simple event. Climates are, in fact, always changing. Between about 1550 and 1850, for example, there was a 'Little Ice Age' when the climate grew steadily colder and 'Frost Fairs' were held on the frozen River Thames. The ice must have reached a considerable thickness to support the activities shown in the picture of the Frost Fair held on the River Thames in the winter of 1683/84.

Figure 4 shows how the climate of Britain changed during the Ice Age, and has changed since. During this period ice advanced and retreated several times. The periods of ice advance are called *glacials* and the periods of ice retreat are known as *interglacials*.

Fig. 3 Frost Fair on the River Thames, 1683/84

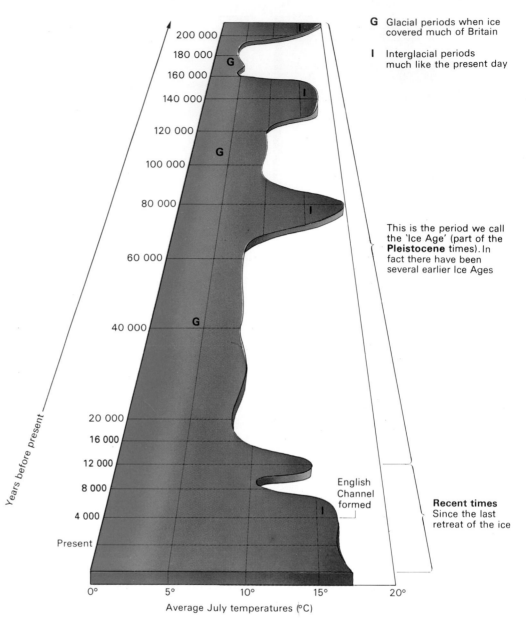

G Glacial periods when ice covered much of Britain

I Interglacial periods much like the present day

This is the period we call the 'Ice Age' (part of the **Pleistocene** times). In fact there have been several earlier Ice Ages

Recent times Since the last retreat of the ice

Average July temperatures (°C)

Years before present

English Channel formed

Fig. 4 Temperature changes in Britain over the last 200 000 years

2 a What length of time, before the present, is shown on the graph above?
b How many times did the ice advance over Britain during the Ice Age?
c When did the last glacial period start, and how long did it last?
d Roughly how much difference is there in the July average temperatures between the glacials and interglacials? (This figure is quite small.)
e The diagram shows that the Ice Age was not just one period of very low temperatures, but a series of comparatively minor temperature fluctuations. From the diagram, would you say that we are still in the Ice Age?

During each of the glacial stages shown in Fig. 4, snow and ice accumulated in the upland areas. The ice then gradually spread further south. Most of the ice, in fact, originated in the higher land of Scandinavia, although there were local, high areas from which the ice advanced in Britain. The final shape of the British Isles was not yet visible at this time. Much of the North Sea was still land (for example, the shallow Dogger Bank fishing grounds), and Britain was still joined to France. The extent of the ice over Britain is shown in Fig. 5. As the last glacial advance was not the furthest, the landscape produced by ice activity is complicated. Landforms are created by one advance of the ice and may be bulldozed by the next.

---

3 Refer to Figs 4 and 5.
a Using an atlas, name the centres of ice dispersion in Britain (numbered 1–7 on the map, Fig. 5).
b When was the English Channel formed? What do you think caused the rise in sea level that brought about this separation of Britain from France?
c By referring to an atlas, describe (using place names) the position of the line marking the limit of the last ice advance over Britain.

The accumulation of ice

In our present climate, any snow that falls in the winter melts during the spring. In highland areas, where the temperatures are lower, there is more snowfall and it takes longer to melt. If the climate were colder than it is now, the winter snowfall would not melt during the spring and summer months but would continue over to the next winter when more snow would fall on top. In this way, snow accumulates on the surface of the land. Figure 6 on p. 60 shows the changes that take place as each year's snow builds up. Air is removed as the ice is compressed. As ice becomes thicker it moves downslope by its own weight.

Fig. 5 Britain in the Ice Age

Ice movement

A mass of moving ice is called a *glacier*. It may move in a valley, like a river, or flow out from a mountainous area across a plain as a 'tongue' of ice (Fig. 7, p. 60). A very broad mass of ice flowing out from its centre in all directions is called an *ice sheet* (or, if smaller, an *ice cap* – see Fig. 1).

A glacier cannot keep growing for ever. It will eventually move into warmer areas where the ice will melt. The length of the glacier may be divided into two parts:

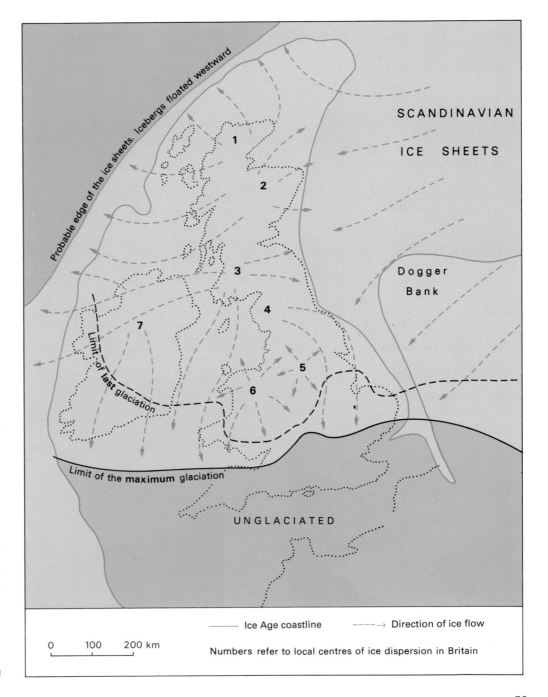

Probable edge of the ice sheets. Icebergs floated westward

SCANDINAVIAN ICE SHEETS

Dogger Bank

Limit of last glaciation

Limit of the maximum glaciation

UNGLACIATED

——— Ice Age coastline   -----→ Direction of ice flow

0   100   200 km

Numbers refer to local centres of ice dispersion in Britain

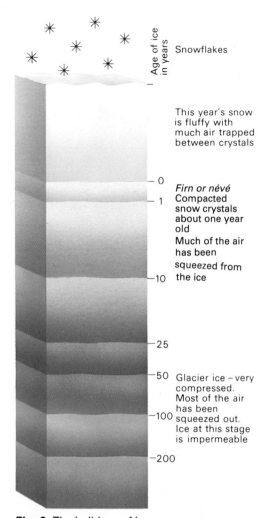

Snowflakes

Age of ice in years

This year's snow is fluffy with much air trapped between crystals

— 0

Firn or névé
Compacted snow crystals about one year old

— 1

Much of the air has been squeezed from the ice

— 10

— 25

— 50 Glacier ice – very compressed. Most of the air has been squeezed out.

— 100 Ice at this stage is impermeable

— 200

Fig. 6 The build-up of ice

Fig. 7 The Gorner glacier, Switzerland

1 the zone where the snow and ice are building up – the *accumulation zone*
2 the zone where ice is melting – the *ablation zone*.

Between these two zones is a line where the rate of accumulation is balanced by the rate of ablation. Figure 8 shows how this line advances (as well as the snout of the glacier) in winter.

The balance between accumulation and ablation is known as the glacier's *budget*. If the rate of accumulation is greater than the rate of ablation then the snout of the glacier moves forwards. If the rate of ablation is greater than the rate of accumulation then the snout of the glacier retreats. Notice though that even if the snout of the glacier is retreating, the ice within the glacier is still moving *forwards*, because melting takes place faster than the ice is advancing.

Although ice is solid it is able to flow. It does this in a combination of ways, depending on the temperature of the glacier:

- by moulding its shape downhill in a plastic way, rather like thick treacle
- by partly melting on the upstream side of rocks in its path and then refreezing once it is past the obstacle
- by slipping over a thin layer of meltwater at its base
- by the movement of fairly solid slabs of ice past each other along lines of faults in the ice.

---

4 Refer to Fig. 9. An expedition was made to find out the pattern of glacier movement. Stakes were driven into the ice in a straight line and their position recorded on a map. The position of the stakes was then examined two months later.
  a Which stake had moved the furthest?
  b How far had it moved?
  c What is the average speed of this glacier, in metres per day and metres per year? The speed of ice varies within the glacier. Like water in a river (see p. 47), the fastest part is away from the sides and bottom.

The variation in the speed of the ice causes stresses within the glacier and cracks or *crevasses* develop. The speed of glacier flow varies within glaciers. It also varies *between* glaciers (from about 100 m to 7 km per year).

The geomorphologist's main concern with glaciers is the way in which they modify the surface of the earth. Like most other landform processes, ice modifies the earth by *erosion* and by *deposition*.

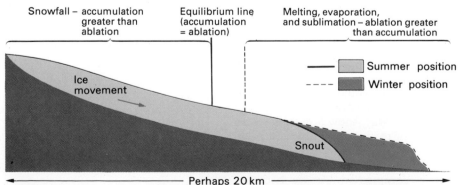

Becoming less cold (lower altitude, latitude)

Snowfall – accumulation greater than ablation

Equilibrium line (accumulation = ablation)

Melting, evaporation, and sublimation – ablation greater than accumulation

Ice movement

Snout

Summer position

Winter position

Perhaps 20 km

Usually highland areas. Mostly landforms of erosion

Landforms in this zone, show both deposition and erosion (ice deposits material and then shapes it)

Usually lowland areas Mostly landforms of deposition

Fig. 8 The glacier's budget

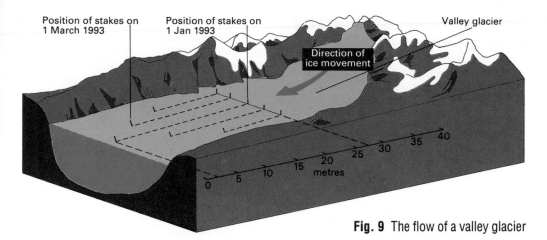

Fig. 9 The flow of a valley glacier

Fig. 10 Striations on rocks after glaciation

Erosion by ice

If the ice moves as slowly as in Fig. 9, where is the power for erosion? It is difficult to get underneath glaciers to see the process at work, so we are not sure precisely how glaciers erode. However, erosion seems to occur as a result of the combination of the following:

- Simple scooping up of material (including soil and loose rocks) that had been weathered before the Ice Age.
- The 'sandpaper effect' of rock particles trapped beneath the ice grinding away the solid bedrock. This process is known as *abrasion*. Deep grooves or *striations* are often left in the surface of the rock, like the scratches made by

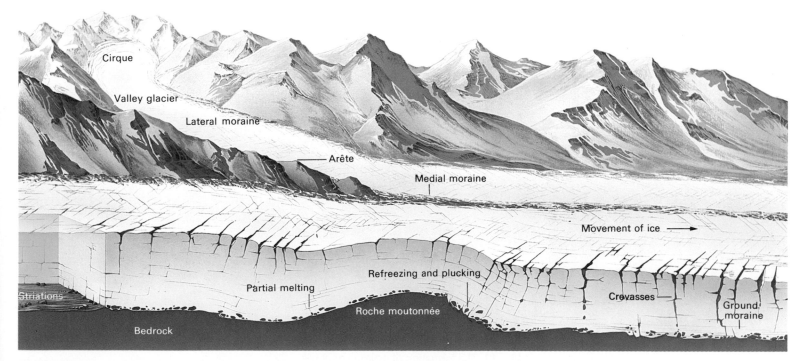

Fig. 11 Glacial erosion and the transport of moraine

REDCAR & CLEVELAND COLLEGE LIBRARY

61

coarse sandpaper on smooth wood. Striations may be seen in areas from which the ice has only recently retreated.

● The removal of rock particles already loosened by jointing. Ice partly melts on the upstream side of rock obstacles in the path of the ice and refreezes on the downstream side. In this way, rock fragments are *plucked* away by the ice.

These three processes may be seen in the section through a valley glacier in Fig. 11.

On the slopes above the surface of the glacier it is likely, in the cold climate, that the temperatures will be varying above and below freezing. There will, therefore, be much weathering by frost shattering, and this loose material may fall onto the surface of the glacier and be carried away. All material transported by the glacier is called *moraine*.

---

5 Refer to Fig. 11.

a How were the following types of moraine formed: *lateral moraine, medial moraine, ground moraine*?

b Examine the landform in Fig. 12. Ice has moved over this mound of rock, passing smoothly over the upstream side and 'plucking' rock fragments from the downstream side. Draw a sketch of this feature and show the direction of the ice movement. Label the diagram with a brief description of both sides. This landform is called a *roche moutonnée*.

Landforms produced by glacial erosion

Most of these landforms consist of features that existed before the Ice Age, but which have been enlarged or otherwise modified by the ice.

Cirques (or corries)

These are large, bowl-shaped hollows in highland areas and are generally the source of ice for glaciers. They vary in size but may be up to 3 km across. They are formed by the gradual accumulation of ice in a hollow in high land. Erosion takes place by freeze/thaw around the patch of ice, and meltwater removes the eroded particles. This is called *nivation*. The ice gradually enlarges the hollow to the shape of a bowl, or armchair – a cirque. Two distinct features of the cirque may be seen after the ice has gone. These are the steep, rocky back wall (often several hundred metres high), and the 'lip'. The back wall was cut progressively steeper either by freeze/thaw activity between the ice and

the rock face, or by plucking away rock fragments broken by jointing. The lip of the cirque may be the result of the rotational slip of the ice. It is formed as the ice erodes less powerfully at the edge of the landform than at the base.

As two neighbouring cirques become enlarged, their back walls may meet back to back, resulting in a steep knife-edge ridge or *arête*. Where three of four cirques cut back on each other, a *horn* or *pyramidal peak* may be formed at the centre (see Fig. 14).

Fig. 14 The Matterhorn – a pyramidal peak

Fig. 12 A roche moutonnée

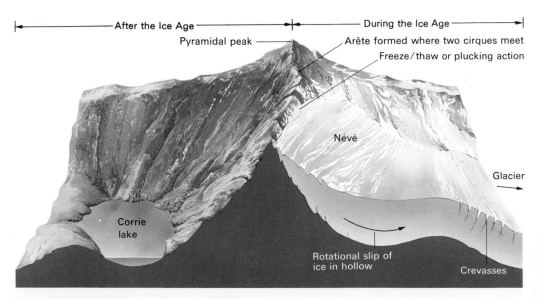

Fig. 13 The formation of a cirque or corrie

Glacial troughs

Ice from the cirques moved down the valleys and joined to form glaciers. The valleys or troughs that were cut by the ice are broad and flat-bottomed, rather like the letter U in cross-section (Fig. 15). They are usually the result of glaciers enlarging pre-existing river valleys. As ice cannot flow so easily around corners as water, the valleys are straightened out and the spurs of the river valleys are planed off or *truncated*. Rivers that flow in glacial troughs today appear too small for the size of the valleys cut by the ice. They are called *misfit streams*. Glacial troughs often contain long, narrow lakes called *ribbon lakes*. (One of these can be seen in the left-hand photograph on p.3.)

The larger troughs had more ice in them, so cut deeper than their tributaries. These tributary valleys were left higher after the ice melted and are known as *hanging valleys*.

Look at Fig.16. A major glacier once filled the large valley in the foreground. It was joined by a tributary glacier at A in the centre of the photograph. During glaciation the area would have looked rather like the scene in Fig. 1.

6 a Referring to Fig. 16, explain the difference between the jagged outline of the mountains above the former level of the ice and the smoother shape of the valleys that were below the ice.

b A stream now flows down this *hanging valley*. What has happened to the stream at B?

c How was the landform at C formed? This feature is known as an *alluvial fan*. What might eventually happen if this process were to continue? (There is a clue in the left-hand photograph on p.3.) How have people used the alluvial fan? Why?

7 Study Figs. 17 and 18 on p. 64 carefully. The photograph shows High Street in the Lake District – an area that displays much evidence of glacial erosion. With the help of the map, copy out and fill in the spaces in the table to the right.

Fig. 15 U-shaped glacial trough

8 Look carefully at Fig. 13, the photographs in Figs 15, 16 and 18, and the left-hand photograph on p.3. From the statements below, draw up two lists headed 'Characteristics of glacial troughs' and 'Characteristics of cirques'.

- Steep rocky back wall
- U-shape in cross-section
- Lip which may hold back lake
- Semi-circular shape
- May contain ribbon lake
- Truncated spurs
- Two cut back on each other to form an arête
- Tributary valleys much higher

Beside each feature, write the place name of an example of that feature.

Fig. 16 A hanging valley: the Upper Inn near St Moritz

Geomorphological name of landform	Place name of landform	Symbol on photograph
Cirque or corrie with corrie lake	Area around Blea Water	
	Upper Riggindale	●
U-shaped valley		■
Arête		
Misfit stream		

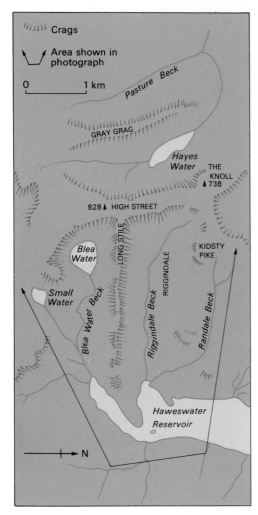

Fig. 17 High Street, Lake District

Fig. 18 High Street and Blea Water, Lake District

Fiords

Fiords are drowned glacial troughs. The glaciers that eroded them reached the coast and the troughs were later drowned by the rise in sea level after the ice melted.

These deep inlets have a ridge or *threshold* at their mouths. This feature is much like the lip of a cirque. Most fiords are on the west coast of countries with high mountains not far inland. This means that when the ice was present the gradient of the glaciers was steep and the erosive power of the glaciers was great. Valleys that existed before the ice were therefore deepened. When the ice reached the sea, however, it melted and became thinner, icebergs broke away, and the erosive power of the glacier was much reduced at the sea's edge. The present fiords, therefore, are deep inlets, although nearer the sea they are comparatively shallow.

Fig. 19 Nordfiord, Norway

Crag and tail features

9 a Look at the diagram of Edinburgh Castle (Fig. 20). Edinburgh Castle stands on a *volcanic plug*. How was this formed? (Check with Chapter 2.) Why is it a good site for a castle?

b Ice moved over this area from the direction shown by the arrow. Much Carboniferous limestone was eroded. Why do you think the volcanic plug was left?

A strip of Carboniferous limestone was protected by the volcanic plug and formed a smooth, moulded ridge. This now lies under the street known as the Royal Mile. The complete feature, of volcanic plug and protected ridge, is known as a *crag and tail*.

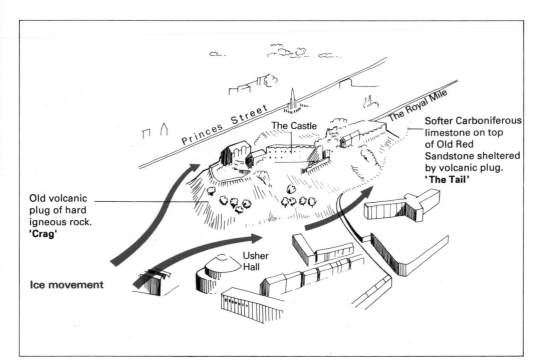

Fig. 20 Edinburgh Castle and the Royal Mile: a crag and tail (diagram and photo)

Deposition by ice

Landforms produced by glacial deposition are very complex. Melting ice deposits moraine mostly at the edges and ends of the glaciers. Later advances of ice bulldoze the deposits of previous advances, re-work them and pile them into new shapes. Deposition takes place in two main ways:

1 Melting ice dumps material on the surface of the land. This rock waste is *unsorted*, which means that large and small rocks, as well as very fine particles, will be jumbled together. This material may be further shaped by more ice passing over it. A covering of unsorted debris such as this on the landscape is known as *till* or *boulder clay*. Its character varies according to the area over which the ice has travelled (and therefore the area from which the material has been eroded).

2 Streams of meltwater flowing from the snout of the glacier carry away rock waste. This is deposited in front of the glacier by *river* processes. Deposits formed in this way tend to be *sorted*.

This means that sands and gravels are arranged in layers as the streams have deposited first the larger and then the smaller particles. Rivers flowing away from glaciers often drop so much material that their course is split into many channels. This is known as *braiding*.

The heap or ridge of debris dropped at the snout of a glacier is known as a *terminal moraine*. These features vary from a few metres to hundreds of metres in height, and in Britain they tell us where a glacier or ice sheet used to end. Part of the city of York is built on a terminal moraine.

Drumlins

10 Describe the surface of the land in Fig. 22. Each of the hummocks is a *drumlin*. They are formed from boulder clay which has been deposited by the ice but shaped while the ice was still moving. The end facing the ice is more blunt than the other, tapering end. Can you see from the photograph which end is which? The ice moved from left to right.

Drumlins rarely occur singly – they are usually found in *swarms*.

Fig. 22 Drumlins

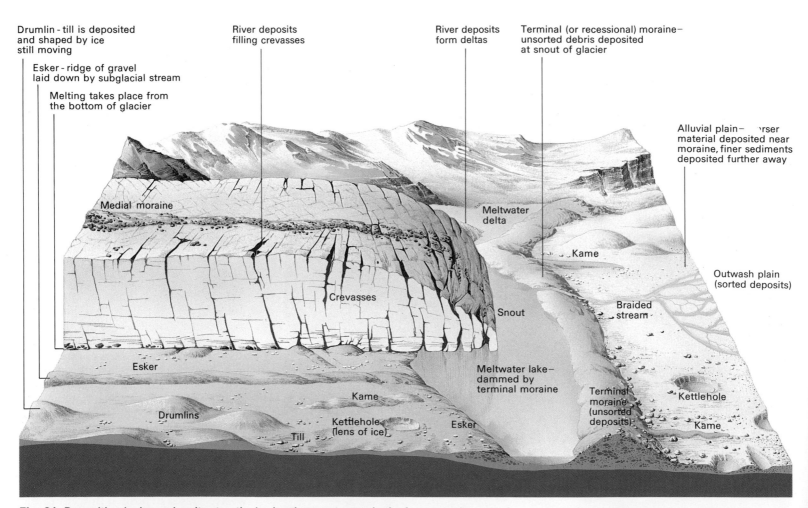

Drumlin - till is deposited and shaped by ice still moving

Esker - ridge of gravel laid down by subglacial stream

Melting takes place from the bottom of glacier

River deposits filling crevasses

River deposits form deltas

Terminal (or recessional) moraine– unsorted debris deposited at snout of glacier

Alluvial plain– ??rser material deposited near moraine, finer sediments deposited further away

Medial moraine

Meltwater delta

Kame

Outwash plain (sorted deposits)

Crevasses

Braided stream

Snout

Esker

Meltwater lake– dammed by terminal moraine

Kame

Drumlins

Kame

Terminal moraine (unsorted deposits)

Kettlehole

Till

Kettlehole (lens of ice)

Esker

Kame

Fig. 21 Deposition by ice and meltwater: the ice has been cut away in the foreground to reveal the landforms to be found under a glacier

11 Study the aerial photograph of the drumlin swarm at Strangford Lough, County Down (Fig. 23).

a What has happened since the drumlins were deposited?

b Use an atlas to find Strangford Lough. Now look at Fig. 5 on p.59. Which direction did the ice that deposited these drumlins come from?

c Do you think that drumlins are landforms of glacial erosion, or deposition, or both? Why?

Erratics

12 Look at Fig. 24. The geologist is examining a boulder of Silurian rock which is resting on top of the Carboniferous limestone, even though it is an older rock.

a This boulder has been transported to its present position. Why could it not be the weathered remains of a layer of rock previously above the limestone?

b This rock has not been transported by people. What is the only possible natural method of transport?

c Rocks transported in this way are called *erratics*. How could they be of use to geomorphologists investigating the flow of ice across Britain during the Ice Age?

d Refer to the section in Chapter 3 on limestone. Suggest why the limestone has not been weathered so much beneath the erratic.

Early people thought that there was something mysterious about erratics. There are many legends associated with these rocks.

Fig. 23 A drumlin swarm at Strangford Lough, County Down, Northern Ireland

Fig. 24 Dark Silurian boulder resting on light Carboniferous limestone

Fluvioglacial landforms

Outwash plains

Melting ice obviously produces a great deal of water. Figure 21 shows this flowing from the glacier snout as streams. These streams carry away the moraine deposited by the ice and deposit it a second time in front of the glacier snout. As these second deposits are laid down by water, however, they are sorted. Finer material is carried further away from the margin of the ice. Depending on the number of streams and the relief of the area in front of the ice edge, these deposits may build up a large *outwash plain*.

Eskers

Figure 25 shows a long ridge of deposited material. This *esker* runs parallel to the direction of ice flow. Eskers are formed by deposition from streams flowing under the ice (see Fig. 21).

Kames

These are made up of sorted debris which has been washed into crevasses in the stagnant ice. As the ice melts, this debris is dumped on the ground. They may also be formed by the build-up of deltas in lakes at the ice margin. Figure 26 is a photograph of a kame in the Glaven Valley in Norfolk.

Fig. 25 An esker

Kame terraces

When lakes at the margin of the ice become completely filled with sediments, a kame terrace may be left when the ice retreats. They may also be formed by deposition along a stream following the edge of the glacier.

Fig. 26 A wooded kame in the Glaven Valley, Norfolk

6 | Coasts

The action of the sea

The power of nature to shape the land is very clearly seen along our coastline. Inland most features alter so slowly that the change is hardly noticed, but this is not so along the coast. On some stretches of coast, landslips happen every year, and there are daily variations in the shape of many beaches.

Waves

Waves are the cause of most of these changes. They form as a result of the wind blowing over the sea and ruffling it up. The stronger the wind is, the bigger the waves. Large waves also occur when the wind has blown for a long distance over the sea. In the same way, if you look at a pond on a windy day you will notice that the waves gradually increase in size as they move across the surface. The further they are from the up-wind side of the pond, the larger they become. The length of water over which the wind has blown is called the *fetch*.

Fig. 2 Axes for plotting fetch against wave height

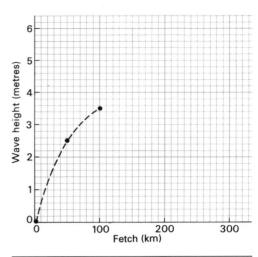

1 Plot a graph to show how the fetch influences the size of waves by completing Fig. 2 using the information in the table.

Fetch (km)	Wave height (metres)
50	2.4
100	3.5
150	4.2
200	4.6
250	4.9
300	5.1

These figures assume that the wind is blowing at 10 km an hour and that the wind has been blowing for at least 20 hours.

2 Use an atlas map of Britain to find the locations of Whitby and Dover. Then, using a map of Western Europe, measure the distance of fetch
a at Whitby from the north and south-east
b at Dover from the south-east and from the east.
Which place is more exposed to large waves?

At Whitby one would expect the largest waves to come from the north because of the long fetch in that direction. The largest waves at a place are called the *dominant* waves, and we shall see that these are very important for moving sand and pebbles along the coastline.

Fig. 1 Start Bay, South Devon

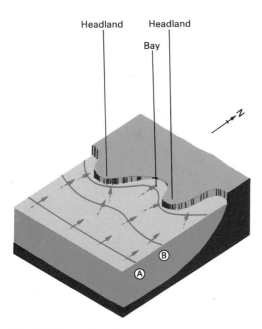

Fig. 3 Wave refraction

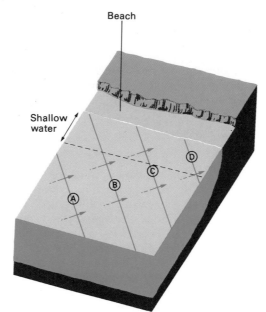

Fig. 4 It is unlikely that waves would move along a beach like this

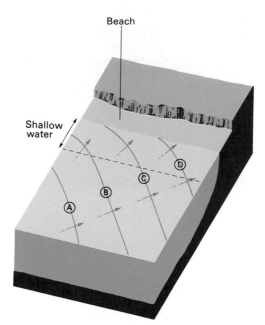

Fig. 5 It is more likely they would be bent like this

The behaviour of waves out at sea may be compared with the waves that pass along a rope if you hold one end and flick it up and down. The shape of a wave moves along the rope, but the rope itself does not move away from you. In the sea it is the shape of the wave that is moving forwards rather than the sea itself. If you watch a piece of wood floating in deep water you will notice that it is not carried forwards by the wave. It just bobs up and down with slight forwards and backwards movements as the wave passes under it.

When waves approach the shore, however, they are affected by the sea floor and behave in a different way. In shallow areas they move more slowly than they do in deep water. This has an important effect which is known as *wave refraction*. Study Fig. 3, which shows a wave approaching the shore. At A it is straight, but soon after this it runs into shallow water off the headlands. It slows down there, but keeps moving forwards at its original speed into the bay. So when the wave reaches B it is no longer straight. Indeed, by the time it reaches the land it is approaching almost directly onto the coast wherever you are.

You may have noticed the results of wave refraction when you have been at the seaside. It is very unusual for waves to travel along a beach in the way shown by Fig. 4. Instead, the waves are bent round as they come into the shallow water (Fig. 5) so that they seem to be coming from almost straight out to sea.

3 Draw a map of the coastline shown in Fig. 3. Then mark in the position of a wave at three different times, assuming it was coming from the south-west rather than from the south.

When a wave moves into really shallow water the sea floor interferes with its movement. The wave then topples over or *breaks*. This happens when the depth of the sea is about the same as the height of the wave. From this moment on it is no longer only the shape of the wave that is moving forwards but the wave itself – as any surf-boarding enthusiast will tell you. Most of the erosion and transport of material along the coast is carried out by the massive power of waves when they have broken.

Tides and currents

The influence of waves is greatly increased by the effect of the *tide*. The level of the sea moves up and down once every 12½ hours. This means that the waves can act on the coast for up to five metres above and below the average (mean) sea level. Tides are caused by the pull of the moon's gravity. The sun's gravity also has a small effect so when both sun and moon pull in the same direction the high tides are higher and the low tides lower than usual. These are called *spring tides*. When the sun and moon are pulling in different directions the range between high and low tides is less (*neap tides*).

Tides are important in allowing the sea to attack a greater area of the coastline because of the vertical movement of the sea every day. They are also the major cause of *currents* around our coasts. These are areas of moving water which may be very wide and slow like the Gulf Stream and North Atlantic Drift (see Fig. 31 on p.100) – the results of winds rather than tides – or much narrower and more local. They are of great importance to sailors, who can be carried many kilometres off course if they do not know the way the currents move. They are less important than waves to the geomorphologist for they mainly carry fine mud rather than the sand and pebbles that waves can move. But their influence should not be forgotten in estuaries and other narrow passages along our coast where vast currents of water move in and out with the tide. For example, a tidal current flows through the Menai Straits (between Anglesey and the mainland of North Wales) at a speed of 15 km/hour, and fast currents are also found at the mouths of the Teign and Dart estuaries in south Devon (Fig. 6). These currents can result in daily changes to the shape of mud flats – a matter of interest to both geomorphologists and sailors.

Erosion

How the sea erodes

The sea erodes the land by *abrasion, hydraulic action* and *solution*. On a stormy day the crash of stones as they are hurled against the rocks shows the power of large waves. At such times the stones themselves are rounded by the process of *attrition*.

---

4 Revise the meaning of the terms *abrasion, hydraulic action, solution* and *attrition* (p.48).

Another powerful form of erosion occurs when waves break against a cliff where air is trapped in joints or hollows. The air is greatly compressed and this enlarges the crack. When the wave retreats the air expands with explosive force, weakening the rock still further.

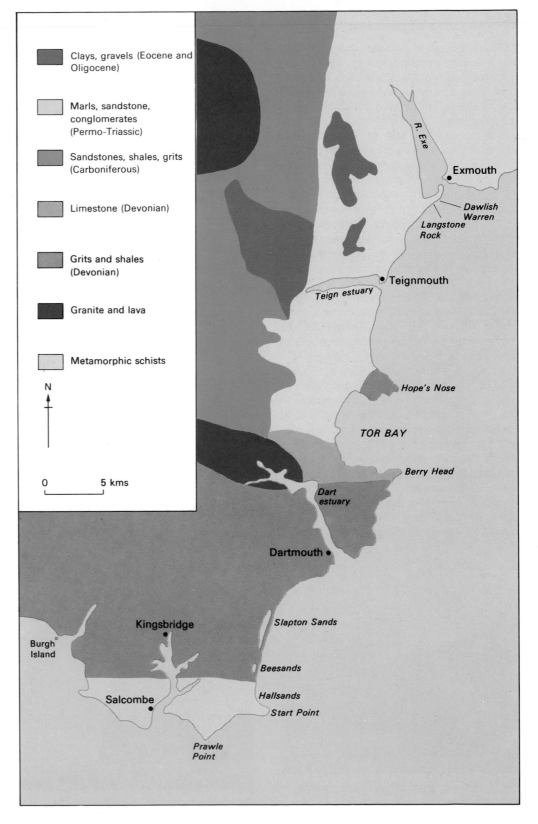

Fig. 6 Map of the South Devon coast

Clays, gravels (Eocene and Oligocene)

Marls, sandstone, conglomerates (Permo-Triassic)

Sandstones, shales, grits (Carboniferous)

Limestone (Devonian)

Grits and shales (Devonian)

Granite and lava

Metamorphic schists

N

0   5 kms

R. Exe
Exmouth
Dawlish Warren
Langstone Rock
Teignmouth
Teign estuary
Hope's Nose
TOR BAY
Berry Head
Dart estuary
Dartmouth
Kingsbridge
Slapton Sands
Burgh Island
Beesands
Hallsands
Salcombe
Start Point
Prawle Point

The results of erosion

Erosion is most important where the land is exposed to powerful waves. These cut a *notch* in the rocks near to high tide level (Fig. 7) and as this is enlarged a steep rock face or *cliff* will be formed if the sea is eroding a highland area. Steep cliffs often occur where erosion is fast because in such places the sea undermines the cliff rapidly, forming a large notch which leads to the collapse of the cliff above. Where the sea erodes less actively, the cliff face is worn back by weathering and is more gentle.

The type of cliff depends on the geology of the coast as well as on the speed of erosion. Impressive cliffs are generally found in areas of hard rocks or in places where the rock contains vertical joints. The famous White Cliffs of Dover are chalk cliffs following vertical joints in an area of active erosion. The angle of dip of the rocks may also influence the steepness of the cliff (Fig. 8).

In areas where soft rocks are being eroded, the collapse of cliffs into the sea may result in the loss of many hectares of land each year. Farmland, footpaths, and even buildings are destroyed in this way. On the Holderness coast of Yorkshire, where there are boulder clay cliffs, about two metres of land a year are being eroded away. This amounts to the disappearance of a strip of land several kilometres wide since Roman times, including not only farmland but entire villages.

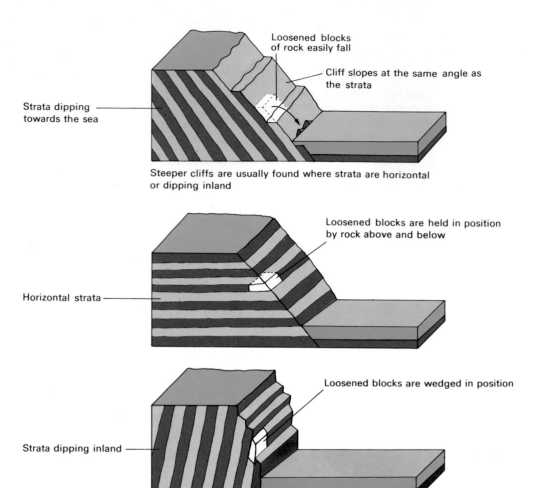

Fig. 8 The steepness of cliffs may be influenced by the angle of dip of the rocks

Fig. 7 Waves cut a notch in the rocks near high tide level

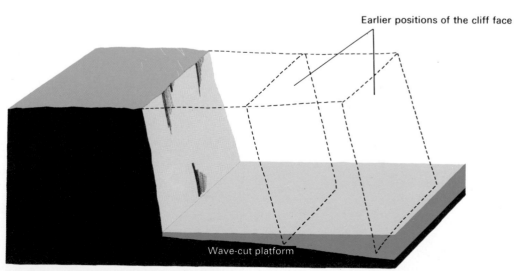

Fig. 9 The formation of a wave-cut platform

Where cliffs are 'retreating' in this way, the rocks that were previously underneath the cliffs are exposed to the sea and eroded by it into a *wave-cut platform*. Figure 10, a photograph taken at low tide, shows a large wave-cut platform below chalk cliffs at Flamborough, in Yorkshire.

Fig. 10 Wave-cut platform at Flamborough, North Yorkshire

Inspection of a cliff face often reveals features that result from the erosion of lines or zones of weakness in the rocks. The sea is particularly good at picking these out. Where the waves enlarge a joint or fault, a cave may form. Air is then trapped and compressed inside the cave and may force its way up cracks to the cliff top. If you were standing at such a point on the cliff top you could put your hand by the crack and feel a blast of air and spray coming out each time a wave crashed into the cave below. Such a feature is called a *blowhole*. Figure 11 shows a blowhole at Flamborough Head, much enlarged by the collapse of part of the cave roof.

If a cave grows in length across a narrow headland it may eventually extend all the way through or meet with another cave on the other side. When this happens the cave, now open to the air at both ends, is known as an *arch*. Figure 12 shows an arch at Langstone Rock, Devon. Notice how the arch has formed where erosion has picked out the line of a fault.

At a later stage, if the roof of an arch collapses, part of the narrow headland becomes a small island, known as a *stack* (Fig. 13). Some stacks are spectacular high rocks, while others have been worn away for many years and can only just be seen above the sea.

Fig. 11 Blowhole at Flamborough, North Yorkshire

Fig. 12 An arch: Langstone Rock, Devon – the arrow indicates the fault line

Fig. 13 A stack: Freshwater Bay, Isle of Wight

Bays and headlands

When the sea erodes a stretch of coastline it not only picks out the joints and small-scale weaknesses in the rocks but also attacks weak areas on a larger scale. If we look at the coastline shown in Fig. 6 we notice that there are several *headlands* – areas extending out into the sea – and between these are *bays* where more of the land has been worn away. Headlands tend to be formed where there are harder rocks which resist erosion by the sea.

5 a Name the headlands in south Devon where the coast is formed of resistant granite and lavas.
b Explain why a bay has been formed between Hope's Nose and Berry Head.

This type of coastline, with distinct bays and headlands, often occurs where bands of hard and soft rock meet the coast more or less at right-angles. It is known as a *discordant* coastline. 'Discord' means disagreement, and the coast is given this name because it cuts across the line of the rocks rather than following them. Where rocks and coastline lie parallel to each other, the coast tends to be much straighter and is known as a *concordant* coastline, 'concord' meaning agreement.

6 Study Fig. 14.
a Which stretch of coast is concordant and which is discordant?
b Look at the pattern of bays and headlands. Which rocks do you think are hard and which are soft?

Erosion and people

Where beaches or cliffs are being rapidly eroded, people are likely to be very concerned, especially where farmland, holiday beaches, or houses are involved. So in several parts of the country large sums of money are spent on *sea defences*. Sometimes a *sea wall* – a concrete cliff – is built to protect the land from erosion. Another way of protecting the coast is to build *groynes*, wooden fences running down a beach into the sea. These keep the sand or

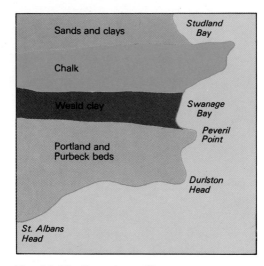

Fig. 14 The Dorset coastline

Fig. 15 Groynes protect the coast

Fig. 16 Derelict cottages at Hallsands, Devon

shingle in place and, by maintaining a larger beach, prevent waves from attacking the cliffs behind.

It is very easy to upset the balance between erosion and deposition along a stretch of coastline. Figure 16 shows derelict fishing cottages at Hallsands, in Devon. In the nineteenth century the boats used to be kept on a beach which lay between the houses and the sea. But in 1897, 650 000 tonnes of shingle were dredged from the sea bed a few kilometres out to sea. This shingle was used to extend the naval dockyard at Devonport, but its removal resulted in waves attacking the beach at Hallsands more vigorously. In a few years the beach had disappeared and the waves then proceeded to erode the rocks on which the houses were built. Within 20 years the village was abandoned.

Transport and deposition

Longshore drift

Water moving up the beach after a wave has broken is known as *swash*. When waves are breaking at an angle to the beach the swash moves not only up the beach but also slightly along it. This water then runs straight down the slope of the beach into the sea. It is then known as the *backwash*. So a pebble picked up at the water's edge by the swash and returned by the backwash would end up a short distance along the beach. This movement of material, which occurs on all but the calmest days, is called *longshore drift*.

Demonstrating longshore drift   **P**

If you are able to visit the coast, place a number of small, brightly painted pebbles at the water's edge. Note whether the waves are approaching the beach from straight out to sea or at an angle. See whether the pebbles are moved along the beach in one direction or whether they are scattered at random in both directions. Explain the movement of the pebbles in terms of the wave direction you noted.

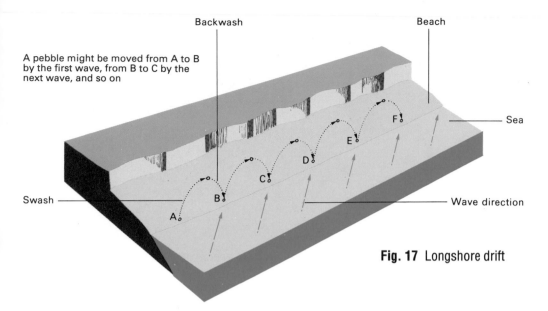

A pebble might be moved from A to B by the first wave, from B to C by the next wave, and so on

Backwash

Swash

Beach

Sea

Wave direction

Fig. 17 Longshore drift

Suggestions:

- A large number of pebbles is needed for this exercise, as some will be dragged out to sea or be buried in the beach.
- Remember that large pebbles will not be moved if the waves are small.
- It is a good idea to pick up the pebbles at the end of the exercise and take them away with you, leaving the beach as tidy as possible.

The direction of longshore drift on any one day is decided by the direction of the waves approaching the shore that day. But if a beach is studied for a period of several years, it is clear that there is an overall movement of material in one particular direction. You will notice that in Fig. 15 there is more material on the right-hand side of the groyne than there is to the left. This is because longshore drift is generally moving the pebbles from right to left and they have built up on the right-hand side of the groyne. The overall direction of longshore drift is determined by the direction of the dominant waves approaching the shore.

7 Revise the idea of *fetch* and how this determines the direction of the dominant waves. Then study an atlas map of the British Isles and work out the direction of longshore drift you would expect to find:

a in East Anglia between Yarmouth and the Thames estuary
b along most of the south coast of England.

Spits, bars and tombolos

The movement of material along the coast by longshore drift is interrupted where an estuary cuts across the coastline. Material gathers at the side of the estuary and over the years this area of deposition grows in length as fresh material is added to it by longshore drift. Gradually it is extended outwards into the estuary, forming a *spit* – a finger-like area of deposited sand or shingle. Some material is removed from the end of the spit by waves and tidal currents. The spit grows when the input of material by longshore drift is greater than the amount removed from it. When the input and output (p. 7) are the same, the spit stops growing. Many spits continue the direction of the coastline across a bay or estuary in this way, though sometimes they leave the coast at a slight angle. This is because they tend to form at 90° to the direction from which the dominant waves are coming.

Figure 18 shows Dawlish Warren, a spit at the mouth of the Exe estuary. It is 2 km

Fig. 18 Dawlish Warren, a spit at the mouth of the River Exe, Devon

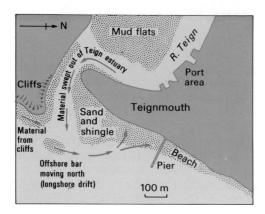

Fig. 19 An offshore bar at Teignmouth, Devon

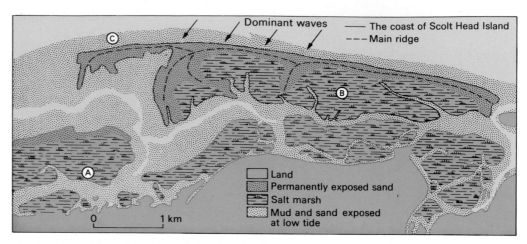

Fig. 20 Map of Scolt Head Island showing the direction of dominant waves

long and has several features typical of spits around the British coast. Notice how it curves round at the bottom of the photograph. Here, at a distance from the land, the sand is more easily forced towards the land by the waves.

Behind Dawlish Warren lies an area of *salt marsh*. Mud is deposited in this area, which is protected from the large waves of the open sea by the spit. As the water becomes shallower, mud is exposed at low tide and special types of marsh vegetation start to grow. Eventually the area is only flooded at spring tides or during storms, and may be used as pasture land. Salt marsh is often broken up by small muddy creeks which are occupied by water at high tide.

On the spit itself, sand blown up from the beach has gathered as *sand dunes* – hills of sand held in position by special long-rooted grasses such as *marram grass*. Dunes that have no grass growing on them change shape according to the strength and direction of the wind, so in many such areas marram grass has been deliberately planted to prevent erosion of the dunes.

Spits often change shape over short periods of time. One storm can completely alter the end of a spit or even break through it where it is narrow. There are also longer-term changes, sometimes the results of human activity. At Dawlish Warren the spit has been badly eroded over the last hundred years. It is thought that the

railway built along the coast south of Dawlish in 1846 has protected the cliffs from erosion. Less material has therefore been supplied to the spit by longshore drift – in other words, the input has decreased. As a result more material has been eroded than has been added to the spit.

Another depositional feature, 9 km further south along the Devon coast, is shown in Fig. 19. It is an *offshore bar*, consisting of a sandbank built up from material carried into the sea by the River Teign and moved along the coast by longshore drift. As it is exposed above the sea only at low tide and is constantly changing its position, it is a hazard to ships entering the Teign estuary. In some parts of the country there are larger offshore bars, exposed at all stages of the tide. One of the largest is Scolt Head Island off the north Norfolk coast.

---

8 Study Fig. 20.

a Explain why salt marsh has grown up at A and B but not at C.

b In which direction does longshore drift move material along the bar?

c 'Scolt Head Island has grown in a series of spurts. When its length has remained the same for some time its seaward end has been forced to curve round inland.' What evidence on the map might be used to support this statement?

A *baymouth bar* is a finger of deposited material which, unlike a spit, completely crosses a bay from one side to the other. Slapton Sands in Devon is a well-known example (Fig. 21). The bar is part of a shingle beach which extends 7 km northwards from Hallsands, crossing the mouths of several bays. A large lake – Slapton Ley – lies behind the main bar. It has been partly filled in with mud deposited by streams entering the northern end of the Ley. Some doubt has been expressed about how Slapton Sands formed. Is it a spit that has steadily grown longer until it touches the land at both ends of the bay? Or did it start as an offshore bar, forced inland by waves until it became the feature we see today? An investigation into the origins of the shingle in the bar suggests that the second idea is probably correct.

A similar feature to the baymouth bar is the *tombolo*, a depositional landform connecting an island to the mainland. The most famous example in Britain is Chesil Beach, and in Fig. 22 you can see the similarity between this feature and Slapton Sands. Both are long, narrow shingle ridges with a lagoon of calm water between the ridge and the former coastline. Rather more common are small tombolos only a hundred metres or so in length such as that at Bigbury-on-Sea, Devon (Fig. 23). Burgh Island may be reached from the mainland at low tide when the tombolo is exposed above sea level.

Fig. 21 Slapton Sands

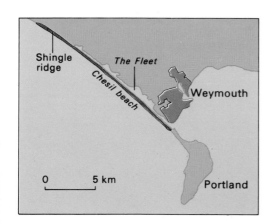

Fig. 22 Chesil Beach

Fig. 23 (a) A tombolo: Burgh Island

(b) Map of Burgh Island

Beaches

The depositional feature that is most familiar to us is the *beach*. The largest beaches are usually found in sheltered bays rather than at headlands where erosion is more common than deposition. The size of a beach from back to front is determined by its gradient. The widest beaches often consist of fine mud, and these slope very gently into the sea. Sandy beaches usually slope more gently than shingle beaches. So as a general rule we can say that the larger the material making up a beach, the steeper it tends to be. Sometimes this is clearly seen on a single beach. There may be a steep ridge at the top of the beach consisting of stones thrown up by storms, especially at spring tides. Lower down the beach more gently sloping sand may be exposed as the tide goes out.

Investigating beach profiles 🅿

If you are visiting a beach, as well as studying longshore drift (pp.74–5) you could also see whether the ideas expressed above apply to that particular beach. Is it true to say that the larger the material making up a beach, the steeper it tends to be? You need a clinometer and a pair of calipers for this exercise – they can easily be 'home-made'.

1 Select a number of places on the beach which have different gradients and consist of different materials. (Or you may have to visit several beaches to get sufficient variety.)

2 At each place measure (a) the steepest gradient and (b) the average size of the material. If the particles are too small to be measured, class them as *mud*, *sand* or *shingle*.

3 Draw a graph similar to the one on this page, and see whether the statement about beaches is true.

Clinometer

Calipers

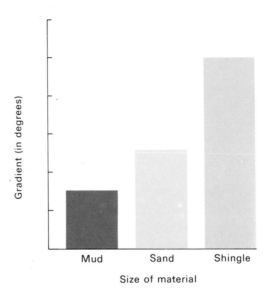

Fig. 24 Graph to show size of material on different beach gradients

Features such as ridges on a beach are the result of the work of waves. A change in the direction or size of the waves results in changes to the shape of the beach. The beach and the waves are part of a system (p.7) and if one part of the system changes (or gets out of balance), the rest of the system will change in response to it. So on some days waves will build up the beach while on others they will drag material away down to the sea. Ridges on the beach may appear and disappear in only a few days. These changes in gradient from day to day make beaches a fascinating place for the student of landforms as well as for the holidaymaker.

7 | Deserts

The desert environment

1 Before you read this chapter or look closely at the photographs and diagrams, write down 10 words that come into your mind when you think of 'deserts'. The most common words could be collected from the class to give a group impression of what deserts are like.

Fig. 1 A popular image of the desert!

It is likely that words such as 'sand', 'Bedouin', 'camels' and 'oases' appeared in your list or that of your class. Most people's impressions of deserts are strongly influenced by the sand dunes of the Sahara or by popular images such as that in Fig. 1. The Sahara is one of the sandiest deserts in the world and yet, as the following figures show, only about quarter of the desert surface is covered with dunes. Most of the desert is rocky or stony.

Type of desert surface	Area of Sahara Desert (%)
Desert mountains	45
Sand dunes	28
Salt crust	12
Bare rock floor	10
Old volcanoes	3
Stony surface	2

The deserts of the world are very dry or *arid*. Some parts of the Atacama Desert in South America, for example, have never had rainfall recorded. Generally, deserts are those areas receiving less than 250 mm of rainfall per year, but low rainfall alone does not make a desert. More important is the relationship between rainfall and temperature, as this determines the amount of evaporation that takes place. Deserts are areas where evaporation is greater than rainfall. The rocks in deserts may reach temperatures during the day of up to 70°C, although at night the temperatures may fall rapidly.

Rainfall in desert areas is very variable. The average annual rainfall at Biskra, Algeria, for example, is 150 mm, yet more than 200 mm fell in a two-day storm in September 1969. Obviously, with such freak storms, average rainfall figures are very misleading.

Rainfall is also variable from place to place within the desert region. Not all parts of even a small area will get equally wet from the passage of one storm.

2 Study the map of the world's deserts (Fig. 2).

  a On an outline map of the world, label the following:

    Gobi Desert (Mongolia)
    Sahara Desert (North Africa)
    Namib and Kalahari Deserts (South Africa)
    Arabian Desert
    Iranian Desert
    Thar Desert (India)
    California Desert (North America)
    Atacama Desert (South America)
    Gibson and Simpson Deserts (Australia)

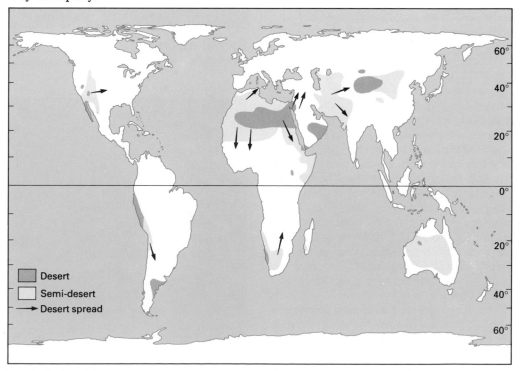

Fig. 2 The world's deserts

Desert
Semi-desert
Desert spread

b With the exception of the Gobi Desert, between which lines of latitude do these deserts lie?

c Estimate the percentage of the earth's surface that is covered by desert or semi-desert. Your answer should show you why a study of deserts is important to geo-morphologists.

Weathering and the desert surface

Deserts are very varied in appearance. The great seas of sand in North Africa and Arabia are known as *erg* desert (see Fig. 3). The name *reg* is often given to the vast stony surfaces of North Africa where wind has blown away finer sand leaving a barren expanse of pebbles (Fig. 4). The evaporation of ground water produces hardened crusts of salt near the surface. Wind and weathering combine to bring a range of reddish colours and strange shapes to the desert landscapes, but many of the landforms, although striking in appearance, are quite rare. Some have become well known simply because they stand out in an otherwise featureless environment.

When rocks are heated by the sun they expand. As they cool they shrink. The strain causes rocks to split. This is a type of physical weathering (see p. 26). Other types of weathering do take place in deserts, although as there is less water present, chemical weathering is not as obvious as in more humid areas. Nevertheless, the small quantity of water that there is plays an essential part in the weathering process in deserts. Dew often forms near the ground and so chemical weathering may be active in hollows or at the base of rock outcrops. This can cause the weathering of softer bands of rock near the ground, sometimes forming *mushroom rocks* (Fig. 5).

Another type of weathering important in hot deserts is the growth of salt crystals in rock. As the desert temperatures are high, water in the rocks evaporates rapidly leaving crystals of salt to grow near the surface. As the crystals expand they force the

Fig. 3 Sandy desert

Fig. 4 Rocky desert

Fig. 5 Mushroom rocks

rocks apart, in the same way that ice does in freeze/thaw weathering.

Generally, as weathering is slower in deserts, the layer of weathered rock fragments (the *regolith*) is shallower.

Water in deserts

Although there is little water in deserts, many of the features of erosion are formed by water. Many deserts have had wetter climates in the past and today's landforms were shaped when there was more water available.

Rivers in deserts differ from those in more humid environments in several ways. The nature of desert rainfall means that the flow of rivers is often irregular. Streams flow when there is rainfall and dry up when there is not. These streams are known as *intermittent streams*. In the event of the freak storms described earlier, torrents of water may rush down valleys which are otherwise dry for many months. Dry valleys that experience these infrequent flows of water are termed *wadis*.

As evaporation rates are high, many rivers do not reach the sea but evaporate in great inland depressions or *playas*. These depressions may cover large areas and become lakes of mud after a sudden storm. They receive not only the solid load of rivers but also the dissolved chemicals. When the water evaporates, the mud dries to produce sun cracks, often in the shape of polygons. Layers of salt are also deposited.

Although desert scenery is very varied, many deserts share the features (shown in Fig. 7) of a mountain mass: a gently sloping rock surface (or *pediment*), and *alluvial fans*.

Pediments appear to be left as the edge of the mountain mass is eroded back. As this happens, remnants of the mountains or plateaus are often left standing.

3 Study Fig. 7 and consider the following facts:

● When a stream passes from an upland area to a lowland area its gradient is reduced.

Fig. 6 A wadi: Tunisia

● River gradient is related to the speed of river flow.
● The speed of a river determines the amount of load it can carry. Describe in detail how alluvial fans form.

4 Study the right-hand photograph on p. 3. This shows all that remains of a plateau surface in Monument Valley, Utah, USA. Flat-topped remnants of the plateau are called *mesas* and those that are too small to have preserved a flat top are called *buttes*. Draw a diagram of this photograph, labelling:

● the sedimentary rock strata
● the screes
● the former plateau surface.

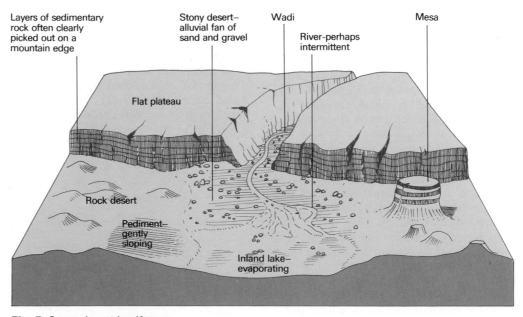

Layers of sedimentary rock often clearly picked out on a mountain edge

Stony desert—alluvial fan of sand and gravel

Wadi

Mesa

River-perhaps intermittent

Flat plateau

Rock desert

Pediment—gently sloping

Inland lake—evaporating

Fig. 7 Some desert landforms

Fig. 8 Ayers Rock, Australia

Figure 8 shows Ayers Rock in central Australia. This sandstone mountain, 350 m high, is a sacred place for Aborigines, and is now also a popular tourist attraction. It is an *inselberg* – an upstanding mass of resistant rock rising sharply above the surrounding *pediment*. It is likely that inselbergs are formed in the same way as mesas.

Landforms produced by wind

Investigating the effects of wind on sand   P

Fill a shallow tray with fine, dry sand. Blow across the surface of the tray (or use bellows). Moisten the sand and blow across the tray again. Describe what happens in both cases.

The wind acts as an agent of erosion, transportation, and deposition in deserts. You may have seen the outside of buildings in cities being cleaned of their surface coating of grime by sandblasting. This method of cleaning uses jets of air with grains of sand in them. The air and sand is directed onto the stonework and the sand scratches away the dirt. Desert winds act as agents of erosion in much the same way. Travellers who have left cars in desert sandstorms have returned to find the paint stripped off by the wind, exposing the bare

metal beneath. Stones on the desert surface may also be polished by the sandblasting. The distinctive pebbles so formed are called *ventifacts*.

It is likely that the action of sandblasting (together with chemical weathering near the surface) helps the formation of mushroom rocks. How much of the shaping of these features is due to chemical weathering and how much to wind erosion probably varies from one place to another. The wind, however, seems to be more important in the formation of *yardangs* (see Fig. 9), as these elongated ridges of rock lie parallel to the direction of the wind.

The Qattara Depression in the Sahara is a saucer-shaped depression about 300 km by 150 km and about 125 m below sea level in the centre. Depressions such as these collect water and therefore the breakdown of rocks by chemical weather-

ing is more common here than elsewhere in the desert. The wind blows away the dry, loosened sand and rock waste and the hollow is deepened. This process is called *deflation*. The Qattara Depression is a large deflation hollow.

---

5 Study Fig. 10.
  a Compare the movement of sand particles by the wind with the transport of load by a river. Describe the size of the particles, the methods and the names given to the processes of transportation.
  b Describe the flight path of sand grains in the zone of saltation.
  c Look at the illustrations of yardangs and mushroom rocks. At what height above ground will erosion be greatest?

The speed of the wind determines the amount of sand it can transport. If small patches of sparse vegetation slow down the wind speed, the wind cannot hold all the sand and so some is deposited. Sand dunes often begin like this.

Dunes are not a haphazard piling up of sand. They often have regular patterns of size, spacing and shape. Sand shapes are usually of three main sizes. *Ripples* are common everywhere in sandy deserts and may be a few centimetres to a metre in height. *Dunes* are from about a metre to about 30 m high. They tend to lie about 100 m to 200 m apart. The largest features are *draa*, up to 300 m high and a kilometre or two apart.

Sand dunes commonly form a regular pattern, known in the Sahara as *aklé*. This pattern is shown in Fig. 11. Wind eddies scoop out hollows and spread out tongues

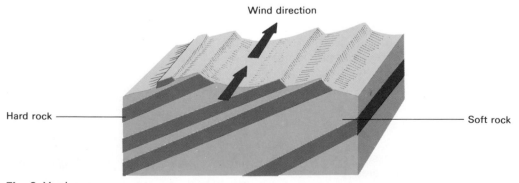

Fig. 9 Yardangs

82

of sand. Less common, but more spectacular, are *seif dunes* and *barchans*.

Seif dunes form in desert areas where the wind blows mainly from one direction but where there are cross-winds. The barchan dune is quite rare and tends to form in areas where the wind blows from one direction only. Figure 13 shows how this type of dune moves.

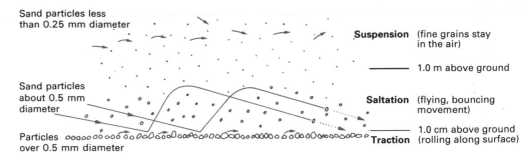

Fig. 10 The transport of sand by wind

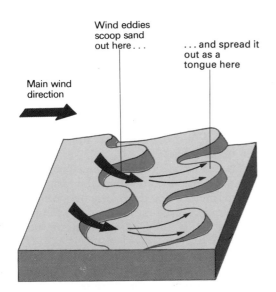

Fig. 11 Aklé pattern of sand dunes

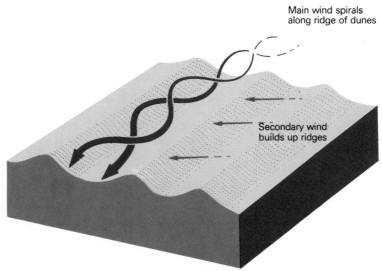

Fig. 12 The formation of seif dunes

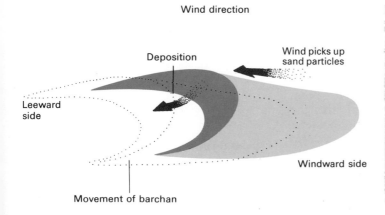

Fig. 13 The formation of a barchan

Fig. 14 A barchan: the Namib Desert

8 Weather and climate

Think about how the weather affects our daily lives. We wear thicker clothes in winter, eat more salads and ice cream in summer, and play different sports with the changing seasons. On a sunny weekend there are more cars heading for the coast, more people in parks, and fewer people staying indoors. Bad weather can cause chaos on the roads and can lead to rising food prices if harvests are bad. Weather forecasts are used by farmers, by the electricity-generating industry, and by building firms for planning their work.

1 Make a list of how weather affects
  a your daily life
  b people's pastimes and hobbies
  c jobs outdoors.

We use the word *weather* when describing changes that happen from hour to hour or day to day. Conditions over a longer period of time are called the *climate*.

Temperature – the driving force

If a car runs out of petrol the engine stops running, before long the headlights go out, and nothing will work. Energy from the petrol provides power for the car. The sun's energy powers the atmospheric 'engine' in a similar way. If the sun stopped shining the wind would die down. Also, sea water would not be evaporated, so there would be no more rain.

The sun's energy, partly in the form of *light*, reaches us by *radiation*. Much of this energy (65%) is reflected back into space or absorbed by the air, so only 45% actually reaches and warms the earth. But the ground does not get hotter and hotter. It is also losing energy. Some disappears into space as longwave radiation. Some is passed on to the lower part of the atmosphere by conduction. Some is used up in evaporating water from the earth's surface.

Recording temperature

Meteorologists – scientists who study the weather – are usually interested in air temperature, although they also provide farmers with information about the temperature of soils. Temperatures vary above different types of surface and change with height above the ground, so weather stations agree to take their temperature readings in a standard way. This is done by keeping thermometers in a *Stevenson screen* (Fig. 1).

Fig. 1 A Stevenson screen

Temperature: local differences

Figure 2 shows the types of thermometer that are kept inside a Stevenson screen. These all work on the principle that the liquid in the *bulb* of the thermometer expands when heated, forcing the *thread* of liquid up a narrow tube. Present temperature is taken from the *dry bulb* thermometer which has a visible mercury thread. The highest temperature since the last set of readings was taken, is recorded by the *maximum thermometer*. This has a

constriction (narrowing) in the thread so that once the mercury has been forced through, it cannot return to the bulb. The length of the thread records the highest temperature, and can be reset by forcing the mercury back into the bulb with a flick of the wrist. It is a larger version of the clinical thermometer used to see whether you have a high temperature when you are feeling ill.

The *minimum thermometer* records the lowest temperature since it was last reset. The bulb contains alcohol rather than mercury. Alcohol is transparent, allowing the observer to see the marker or *index* it contains. When the temperature falls, this index is pulled down the tube by the end of the alcohol thread. It stays at this level when the temperature rises because the expanding alcohol can flow past it. The right-hand end of the index points to the lowest temperature since the last observation. The thermometer is reset by being tilted so that the index floats to the end of the alcohol thread.

The *wet bulb thermometer* usually records a lower temperature than the dry bulb thermometer. The difference between the two temperatures can be used to calculate the *relative humidity* – the amount of water vapour in the air.

You may have come across a type of thermometer that records both maximum *and* minimum temperatures. This is known as a *Six's thermometer*. It is less accurate than separate maximum and minimum thermometers but is much cheaper.

2 Study Fig. 2 and give
  a the present temperature
  b the lowest temperature
  c the highest temperature
  since the thermometers were last observed and reset.

Investigating how temperatures change with height above a tarmac surface on a sunny day **P**

Gently place the bulb of a thermometer against the ground and after a minute or so, take a reading. Then take the temperature at

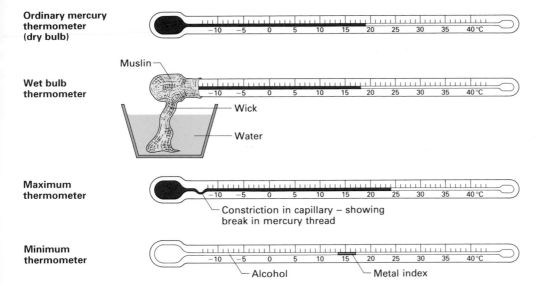

Ordinary mercury
thermometer
(dry bulb)

Muslin

Wet bulb
thermometer

Wick

Water

Maximum
thermometer

Constriction in capillary – showing
break in mercury thread

Minimum
thermometer

Alcohol   Metal index

Fig. 2 Thermometers

heights of 2 cm, 5 cm, 10 cm, 50 cm, 1 m, and 1.5 m. Make sure that the sun does not shine directly onto the thermometer and that you do not warm the bulb of the thermometer with your hand. Plot a graph of the temperature against height.

Investigating how temperatures change over different surfaces [P]

Take temperature readings above different surfaces near your school – above tarmac, concrete, grass, bare earth, and if possible above the edge of a pond. All the readings should be taken within a short space of time, preferably on a calm, sunny day. Compare your readings with those taken by others in your class and see which surfaces can be associated with high or low temperatures.

Different surfaces vary in temperature for three reasons.

1 *They reflect different proportions of the sun's radiation.* For example, snow reflects about 80%, deserts and the sea about 35%, and grass 25%. On a sunny day, dark-coloured surfaces are usually hotter than those of a lighter colour.

2 *They have different specific heat capacities.* The specific heat capacity of a substance is the amount of energy required to raise the temperature of 1 kg of that material by 1°C. A given amount of heat raises a kilogram of sand to a higher temperature than a kilogram of water. Water is particularly slow to heat up, but it is also slow to cool down. Weather forecasters talk of 'cool sea breezes' in the summer. Winds blowing in from the sea are cool

because the water has not warmed up. On a larger scale, the centres of continents are usually hotter than coastal areas in the summer months. The opposite is true in winter, when coastal regions are affected by the warmer sea.

3 *Heat penetrates to different depths.* Again the contrast is clear when temperatures in the water and on land are compared (see Fig. 3). This also explains why the sea warms up slowly.

The *slope* of the earth's surface can also influence temperature, especially when north-facing and south-facing slopes are compared. As a result, opposite sides of a valley may have quite different types of vegetation and farming. Market gardeners particularly favour south-facing slopes, because crops ripen earlier there.

Temperature patterns in the British Isles

Winds from the north generally bring cold weather, while southerly winds usually bring warm weather to the British Isles. Air coming from polar regions brings with it the character of that area – it is a cold *air mass* (Fig. 5). The whole of Britain is sometimes dominated by just one air mass. At other times a cold air mass may cover part of the country whilst other areas are much warmer. On such occasions you will see a *front* marked on weather maps. A front is a line separating air masses with different temperatures.

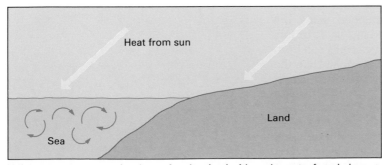

In the sea, water warmed at the surface is mixed with cooler water from below. The heat is spread over a greater depth than on the land

Fig. 3 Temperatures: land and sea

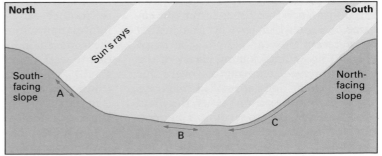

Compare the heating effect of the sun's rays at A, B and C. The heat is much more concentrated on south-facing slopes (in the northern hemisphere)

Fig. 4 Temperatures on different slopes

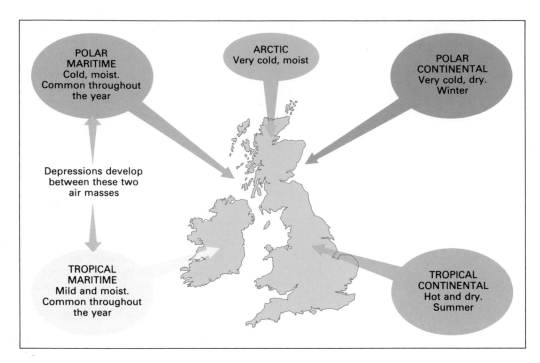

Fig. 5 Air masses affecting the British Isles

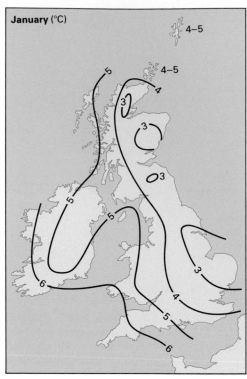

January (°C)

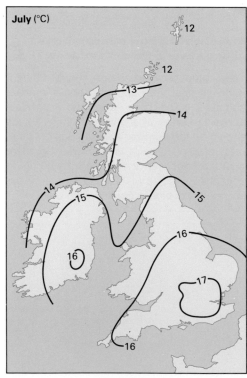

July (°C)

Fig. 6 Sea-level isotherms over the British Isles

3 Over the next fortnight, keep a record of air masses passing over your home area. Note how long each one lasts, whether it is warmer or colder than usual for the time of year, and whether it is wet or dry.

Air masses result in the temperature changing from day to day, and weather forecasters study these when they try to predict temperatures a day or two ahead. But what about looking further into the future? Is it possible to select a part of Britain that is likely to be especially sunny in June, or particularly hot in August? For this information forecasters turn to the *climatic averages* which have been calculated for a recent 30-year period. The maps (Fig. 6) show lines joining places of the same average temperature over this period. These lines are called *isotherms*, and to make comparisons easier, the effect of altitude is taken into account. Temperature decreases as you go up a mountain, so high areas are almost always colder than lowlands. This effect is so strong that it hides other changes of temperature from place to place. We can only see these other variations if the isotherm maps show temperature adjusted for altitude.

4 Describe the pattern shown by (i) the January isotherms (ii) the July isotherms:
a Which parts of the country are particularly warm or cold in each season?
b In which direction does it become warmer in each season?
c Pick out any facts about temperatures in Britain that surprise you.

Temperature variations from one place to another can be explained using the information summarised in Fig. 7. In July the isotherms in Britain generally run from east to west – the north is cooler than the south. The further south you travel (towards the equator), the higher the sun is in the sky. The sun's energy is therefore concentrated on a smaller area, which becomes hotter. If the sun is low in the sky, the same amount of energy has to heat a larger area. This idea is easily illustrated: shine a torch vertically down on the floor, and then shine it down at a gentler angle.

Which lights the floor more brightly? This experiment also explains why it is hotter at midday than at dawn or dusk, and hotter in the summer than in winter.

There is another reason why the north is colder than the south. When the sun is low in the sky, its energy passes through the atmosphere at a shallow angle, so more is lost before it reaches the earth. Even the longer summer days in the north cannot make up for the sun's low angle and poor heating power.

Notice, though, that the July isotherms in Fig. 6 bend north over the land. Coastal areas are cooler because sea temperatures remain relatively low. In January the influence of latitude is less obvious. The isotherms run from north-west to south-east, with the west warmer than the east. There are three main reasons for this:

1 The most frequent (*prevailing*) winds in Britain come from the west. They blow in over an ocean which (because of its specific heat capacity) is warmer than the land in the winter. These winds bring warmth to western Britain but have less influence in the east.
2 The warming influence of westerly winds is increased by a warm ocean current, the North Atlantic Drift. Without this current our temperatures would be 15° lower, there would be glaciers on the higher mountains, and farming would be almost impossible.
3 Cold continental air masses sometimes push into the east while there are warmer maritime air masses in the west.

The pattern of winter temperatures may well surprise you. At sea level the north-west coast of Scotland has warmer winters than the south-east of England. Figure 8 shows subtropical plants growing in a garden at Poolewe – evidence of the mild winters on our north-west coast.

5 Explain why
a summer temperatures are higher than winter temperatures
b southern Britain is warmer than northern Britain in summer
c western Britain is warmer than eastern Britain in winter.

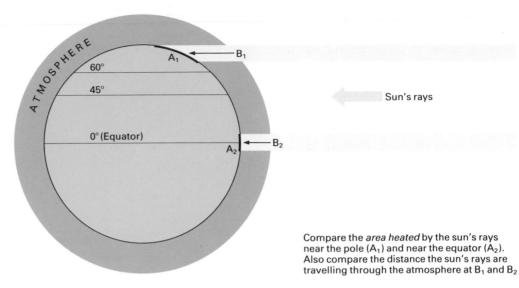

Sun's rays

Compare the *area heated* by the sun's rays near the pole (A_1) and near the equator (A_2). Also compare the distance the sun's rays are travelling through the atmosphere at B_1 and B_2

Fig. 7 Concentration of the sun's rays

Fig. 8 Subtropical gardens at Poolewe in the north of Scotland

Pressure and wind

Air pressure

Some newspaper and television weather forecasts include maps like the one in Fig. 9. The most obvious features on these are the *isobars* – lines joining places of equal pressure. What is air pressure and why is it so important to the meteorologist?

In 1643 Torricelli and Galileo discovered that the atmosphere presses down on the earth with a pressure sufficient to

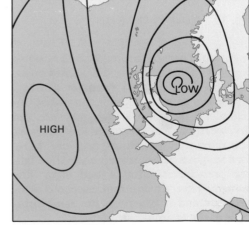

Fig. 9 A weather forecast map

support a 75 cm-long column of mercury in a tube. The *air pressure* varies slightly from day to day, so the column of mercury rises and falls. This gives us an instrument for measuring air pressure – the *mercury barometer*. Mercury is used because it is a dense liquid, and the column is fairly short – a water barometer would have to be 10 m high!

Isobars could be plotted in units of 'centimetres of mercury', but meteorologists actually use the *millibar* (mb). The average air pressure at sea level, 75 cm of mercury, is equal to 1013 mb. Because air pressure decreases with height, the pressure recorded at a weather station is always converted to the value that would have been measured if that place had been at sea level.

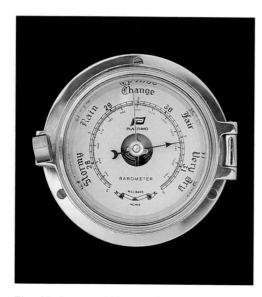

Fig. 10 An aneroid barometer

Another type of barometer is the *aneroid barometer* (Fig. 10). The dial shows pressure, and also gives hints about the weather. There is a general, though somewhat unreliable, link between high pressure and dry weather, and between low pressure and rainy weather. Rising pressure therefore suggests an improvement, while falling pressure is often a bad sign. The *barograph* keeps a continuous record of air pressure and is based on the same principle as the aneroid barometer.

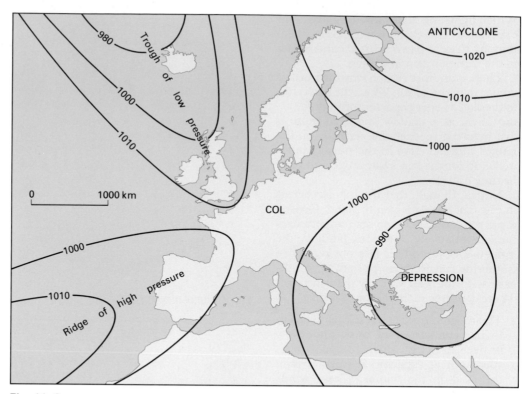

Fig. 11 Common pressure systems over Europe (simplified)

Air pressure varies from place to place and from one day to another. Light, warm air may be rising (*convection*) to give low-pressure areas, or dense, cold air may be sinking and forming high pressure. But most pressure systems are caused by air movements high above the earth. For example, there is a band of fast-moving air, a *jetstream*, circling the earth, and often passing over Britain (see Fig. 30 on p. 99). As this swings from side to side it sucks air up from below, forming areas of low pressure known as *depressions*. Elsewhere it forces air downwards, causing high-pressure areas (*anticyclones*) at ground level. These pressure systems may be recognised from an isobar map (Fig. 11). Between the anticyclones and depressions that pass over Britain guided by the jetstream, are other pressure areas. *Troughs* of low pressure have isobars shaped like valley contours on a relief map. *Ridges* of high pressure extend outwards from anticyclones. The area between several depressions and anticyclones is known as a *col*.

The wind

Air pressure directly affects the direction and speed of moving air or *wind*. Here are two simple rules relating to pressure and wind:

1 The closer together the isobars, the stronger the wind speed.
2 The wind direction can be worked out from the pattern of isobars (Fig. 12).

---

6 a Draw a line at right-angles to the isobars (A–B).

b Put arrows on this line, indicating the direction from high to low pressure (the *pressure gradient*).

c Construct a line at 70° from the line A–B. The wind is blowing along this line from C to D.

Wind direction and speed are shown on some weather maps by symbols called *wind arrows* (Fig. 13). These have 'feathers' on one side, and the 'tip' is actually a circle.

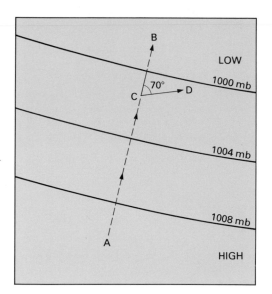

Fig. 12 Relating wind direction to isobars

Fig. 14 An anemometer in use

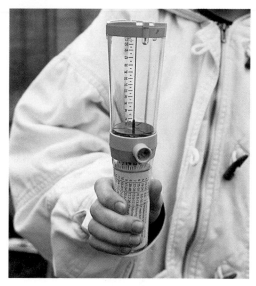

Fig. 15 A simple anemometer

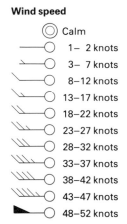

Wind speed

◎	Calm
	1– 2 knots
	3– 7 knots
	8–12 knots
	13–17 knots
	18–22 knots
	23–27 knots
	28–32 knots
	33–37 knots
	38–42 knots
	43–47 knots
	48–52 knots

Fig. 13 Wind arrows

Wind direction is measured by a *wind vane*. Another simple method is to blow soap bubbles and record their movement with a compass. Bubbles can be used to show local variations in wind direction caused by buildings or trees.

Wind speed is recorded with an *anemometer* (Fig. 14). The speed is shown on a dial. A simpler though less accurate instrument is shown in Fig. 15. When using an anemometer it is important to remember that nearby obstacles affect wind speed. Trees slow the wind down considerably. In areas such as the Rhône valley (France),

poplars are planted in lines known as *wind breaks* to provide protection for crops. Though buildings and hills shelter some areas, they can also funnel the wind, creating higher than normal wind speeds.

When an anemometer is not available, wind speed may be estimated using the *Beaufort scale*. This was named after Admiral Beaufort who worked out a similar scale for sailors in the early nineteenth century. The Beaufort scale is used in shipping forecasts broadcast by the BBC.

---

7 a Keep a daily record of wind directions. Make your own observations, and refer to newspaper, TV and radio weather forecasts.

b When you have a month's readings, construct a *wind rose* (Fig. 16). How is your rose different from or similar to Fig. 16? Does your rose support the statement that the prevailing winds in Britain are westerlies (that is, from the north-west, west and south-west)?

Investigating wind speed 🅿

If you can obtain or make an anemometer, investigate the influence of a forest, or of buildings, on the wind speed. This is especially interesting when winds are strong.

● How far into the forest does the wind penetrate?

● How far downwind of a building or forest is the wind slower than you would expect?
● Can you find areas where the layout of buildings results in particularly high wind speeds?

Buildings often change the wind *direction* too, especially by setting up circular patterns (*eddies*). You can investigate these, providing the wind is not too strong, by blowing bubbles and following their directions.

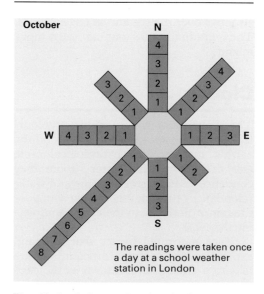

Fig. 16 A wind rose showing the frequency of winds from each direction

REDCAR & CLEVELAND COLLEGE LIBRARY

We have seen that there is a link between pressure and wind. In fact, it is differences in pressure that *cause* winds. The air in a bicycle tyre is under pressure. The air outside is at a lower pressure. If you undo the valve, air flows out of the tyre, from high to low pressure. The atmosphere has areas of high and low pressure but because of the earth's rotation the wind does not blow directly from high to low pressure, at right-angles to the isobars. Instead it blows almost parallel to the isobars, in great swirling patterns. In the northern hemisphere the winds blow anticlockwise around depressions and clockwise around anticyclones. In tropical areas there are strong low-pressure systems called *hurricanes*, and winds around these are very fast. Hurricanes particularly affect the West Indies and southern United States (where they are called *cyclones*), South-east Asia (*typhoons*) and the northern coast of Australia.

Figure 17 is an astronaut's view of a hurricane. The *eye* in the centre is an area of clear skies and gentle breezes. Around this are towering clouds and a massive spiral of winds, often up to 200 km per hour in speed. Hurricanes do terrible damage to crops and buildings on land, while at sea they can sink ships, and cause flooding in coastal areas. Heavy rainfall makes the flooding worse. Hurricanes are most destructive over the sea and in coastal areas. They gradually die out as they move inland.

Clouds

The air contains water vapour, a colourless gas that evaporates from water on the earth's surface. The hydrological cycle (see p.7) shows that water vapour may condense to form small droplets of water (clouds). In turn clouds are the source of the rain which falls to the earth, completing the cycle.

Cloud is formed by air that is rising, expanding and cooling. If its temperature falls to a critical level known as the *dew-point temperature*, the water vapour condenses and clouds form. The base of the clouds shows the height where dew-point temperature is reached (the *condensation level*). There are three main reasons why air may rise and start the process of cloud formation.

1 *Convection* Pockets of warm air form when the ground is heated by the sun. Heated air is less dense, so it moves upwards, producing *thermals*, which glider pilots use to gain height. When the thermals are gentle, cumulus clouds are formed (Fig. 18). Cumulonimbus clouds are the result of stronger thermals. The air can rush upwards at several metres a second – such clouds have been known to lift parachutists up into the top of the clouds instead of allowing them to fall to the earth. Cumulonimbus clouds are a warning to aircraft of turbulent conditions. Passengers are advised to keep their safety belts fastened, as the aircraft may suddenly rise or fall under the influence of strong air currents. One reason for the great height of cumulonimbus clouds is that

Fig. 17 A hurricane viewed from space

Fig. 18 Cumulus clouds

90

heat is released during the process of condensation. This can result in more uplift, more condensation, and so on.

2 *Fronts* Where two air masses of different temperatures meet at a front (p.85), the warm air rises over the cool air. All the clouds illustrated in Fig. 25 on p. 95 are associated with fronts and they often occur in a particular order, as the diagram shows.

3 *Relief* Where air blows over a hill or mountain it may be forced upwards until condensation takes place and clouds form. If a front has to pass over hills, this considerably increases the likelihood of the clouds producing rain.

Clouds come in many shapes and sizes. Their names are put together from these words:

Stratus: a layer cloud, fairly flat at top and bottom.

Cumulus: a cloud where one part is heaped up on another. These clouds may be flat below but are hummocky above. They are sometimes described as looking like cotton wool.

Cirrus: a high-level cloud made of ice crystals rather than water droplets. These clouds are usually thin and some hazy sunshine gets through.

Nimbus: a cloud producing rain or snow.

These terms may be used alone or together to describe the basic cloud types (see Fig. 25 on p. 95).

---

8 Keep a daily record of cloud type and amount. The amount is expressed in *oktas* (how many *eighths* of the sky is covered, for example ⅜ = 3 oktas). Try to decide whether the clouds are forming because of convection, or fronts – you will find weather maps useful for this.

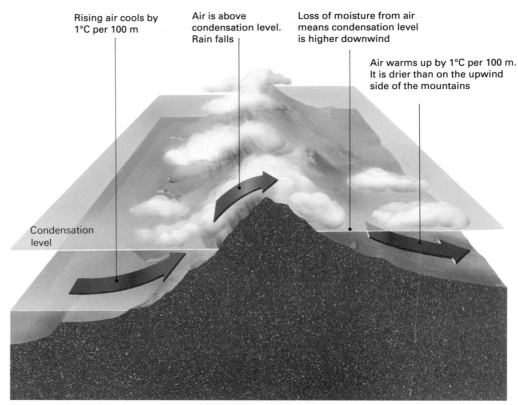

Rising air cools by 1°C per 100 m

Air is above condensation level. Rain falls

Loss of moisture from air means condensation level is higher downwind

Air warms up by 1°C per 100 m. It is drier than on the upwind side of the mountains

Condensation level

Fig. 19 Orographic (relief) rainfall

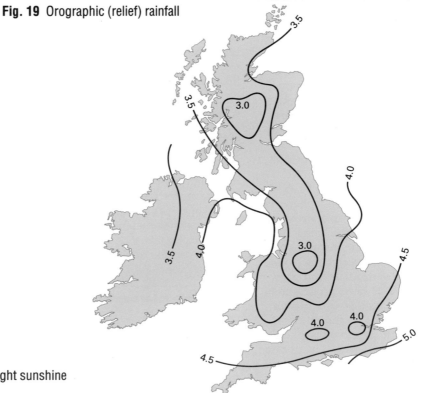

Fig. 20 Average number of hours of bright sunshine daily over the British Isles

The amount of cloud is one of the main influences on how much sunshine an area receives. This is measured by a *sunshine recorder*.

The length of day also affects the amount of sunshine received. In winter the south of England has longer days than the north of Scotland, but in summer the position is reversed.

9 Explain the pattern of sunshine hours shown in Fig. 20.

Precipitation

Clouds do not always produce precipitation (rain, sleet, snow and hail), but when they do it is because of the following processes.

Because temperature decreases with height, the temperatures in clouds above the British Isles are at or below 0°C, even in summer. The clouds are therefore composed of ice crystals or of supercooled water droplets which have not frozen even though they are below 0°C. (In clouds, temperatures may be as low as −30°C before the tiny water droplets freeze.) A cloud consisting largely of these supercooled water droplets is likely to produce snow if ice crystals start dropping through the cloud. When the snowflakes partly melt as they fall through the air they become *sleet*, or *rain* if they melt completely. Most rain in Britain is, in fact, melted snow.

In tropical areas, clouds rise to great heights but because the atmosphere is warm they are usually made up of ordinary water droplets rather than supercooled water or ice crystals. Rain forms when large cloud droplets fall through the cloud, colliding with smaller droplets and growing into raindrops. The same process may occur in low stratus clouds over Britain, but because these clouds are thin the droplets do not have time to grow very large. These small droplets may evaporate before reaching the ground. Otherwise they produce *drizzle* rather than heavy rain.

Measuring rainfall

If a weather broadcast states that '15 mm of rain fell yesterday', it means that if no water had evaporated or drained away, the ground would have been flooded to a depth of 15 mm. The annual rainfall of Birmingham is 730 mm, so it is fortunate that all the water does not, in fact, stay on the surface.

Rain gauges are used to measure precipitation. A gauge must be carefully sited. It should not be placed near buildings or trees which could get in the way of rain slanting down towards the ground. Rain entering the gauge collects in a glass bottle. Each day this is emptied into a narrow measuring jar so that even small amounts of rainfall can be measured accurately. If there is not enough water to transfer into the measuring jar, this is recorded as a *trace* of rainfall. Any snow that gathers in the gauge is melted and the amount of water is measured. One centimetre of snow, when melted, is equal to about one millimetre of rain.

A simple rain gauge can be made very cheaply using a plastic funnel and a milk bottle. You could use this type of gauge for the exercises that follow. Remember to relate the size (area) of the funnel mouth to that of the milk bottle when working out how much rain has fallen.

Setting up a rain gauge   **P**

Measure the diameter of the base of the bottle, halve this to find the radius, and then work out its area. Also calculate the area of the funnel mouth. How much larger is the area of the funnel than the area of the bottle? If it is three times larger, you will have to divide the depth of water in the milk bottle by 3 to get the true rainfall. If possible, sink the base of the bottle into the ground to prevent it from being knocked over.

Measuring intercepted rainfall   **P**

Place several rain gauges under different parts of a tree and another well away from the tree. Compare the average rainfall of the gauges under the tree with that of the gauge in the open. How much of the rain is the tree *intercepting*? Is the proportion similar in both

light and heavy rain? In summer and in winter? In the first half hour, the second half hour, and after the rain? (You may have to get wet – and don't forget that water may continue to drip into the gauges after the rain has finished.) You could also compare the interception rates of different types of vegetation.

Precipitation in the British Isles

If you want a summer holiday in the British Isles with as little rain and as much sunshine as possible, where should you go? Several south-coast holiday resorts claim the best record, each using figures from different years to prove their point. Of course, rainfall is not only of importance to holidaymakers. It influences the crops farmers grow and how successful they are. The pattern of farming in Britain cannot be explained properly without reference to the pattern of rainfall, which has several distinct characteristics (Fig. 21):

1 The prevailing winds come from the west, so that is where most of the rain falls. The further east the winds have to travel, the drier they become.
2 When winds come from the east they tend to be drier because they have passed over a smaller area of sea. The east coast has a relatively low rainfall.
3 Most of the high land in England, Scotland, and Wales lies in the west. This causes *relief* or *orographic* rainfall, and increases the amount of precipitation from fronts as they pass over. To the east of the mountains there is a *rainshadow* effect, where precipitation is less because the air has lost much of its moisture.

Unlike some areas of the world which have wet and dry seasons, Britain gets rainfall throughout the year. In the east of the country there is little variation in the amount of rainfall from one month to the next, if the figures are averaged out over a number of years. The west gets more rainfall in winter than in summer because more fronts come in from the Atlantic at that time of year.

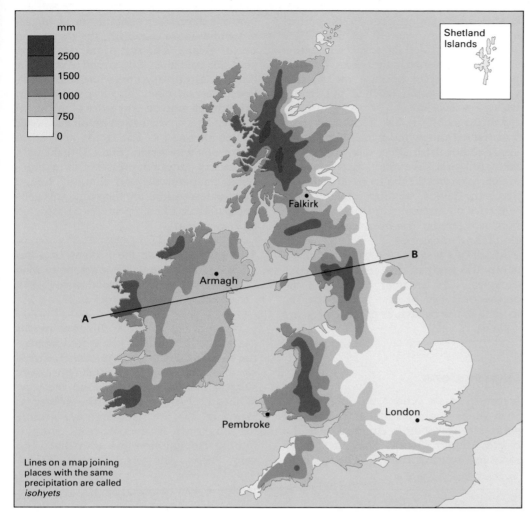

Fig. 21 Mean annual precipitation in the British Isles

Lines on a map joining places with the same precipitation are called *isohyets*

10 Lines on a map joining places with the same precipitation are *isohyets*. On a copy of Fig. 21, draw a cross-section of British precipitation from A to B, as if you were drawing a cross-section from a contour map. Explain the pattern in your diagram.

11 Fig. 22 gives rainfall and temperature figures for Pembroke, Falkirk and Armagh – but you are not told which is which.

a Plot graphs for each of these places and compare your graphs with the graph for London (Fig. 23). Notice that monthly rainfall is shown by bar graphs whereas temperature is shown by a line joining average monthly temperatures.

b Bearing in mind the total rainfall, the distribution of rain through the year, and the pattern of temperature (explained on pp. 85–7), decide which town is represented by each graph. Explain your choice.

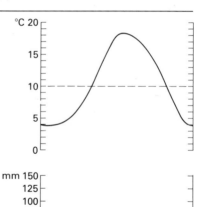

Total precipitation 610 mm

Fig. 23 London: temperature and precipitation

		J	F	M	A	M	J	J	A	S	O	N	D
1	°C	3.7	3.8	5.2	6.9	9.5	12.7	14.7	14.2	12.3	9.1	6.0	4.5
	mm	61	43	41	41	56	48	76	79	64	71	61	53
2	°C	4.6	4.9	6.3	7.9	10.7	13.6	15.2	14.7	12.7	9.7	6.4	5.1
	mm	84	56	51	53	61	61	84	86	74	84	74	79
3	°C	5.8	5.6	6.8	8.8	11.4	14.3	15.8	15.9	14.3	11.3	8.2	6.5
	mm	124	81	69	57	66	53	86	89	91	119	124	122
		Winter		Spring			Summer			Autumn			Winter

Fig. 22 Average temperature and precipitation at three places in the British Isles

Our rainfall is also affected by *air masses* moving over the country. These vary in humidity as well as in temperature (see Fig. 5, p. 86). Continental air gives less rain than maritime air. Some air masses are more *stable* than others. Air coming from the north (especially polar maritime air) moves over warmer land as it crosses Britain, and is warmed at ground level. The air tends to rise and may give rain, and is described as *unstable*. Tropical air on the other hand will probably be cooled at the base, so is less likely to rise and give rain. This is called a *stable* air mass.

Weather forecasts

Forecasting methods

Modern weather forecasting dates back to the mid-nineteenth century when the invention of the telegraph allowed forecasters to put together readings from stations all over the country. They could then draw up charts showing variations in temperature and pressure from place to place. Meteorologists began to recognise the patterns shown on these maps, particularly the anticyclones, depressions and fronts.

In the early twentieth century ships crossing the Atlantic started to send back weather reports and later, special weather ships were stationed in the ocean. This was particularly useful because the weather they reported often reached the British Isles a few days later.

More recently it has been discovered that temperatures and winds high in the upper atmosphere affect our weather, so meteorologists have made increasing use of data from weather balloons and aircraft. Since the 1960s, weather satellites have sent back photographs and other information, while radar has been used to track clouds and rainstorms.

Much of a weather forecaster's skill involves the study of depressions and anticyclones. The amateur as well as the professional can predict the weather by looking at the behaviour of these pressure systems.

Depressions

Depressions, or centres of low pressure, form where warm tropical air meets cold polar air over North America and the North Atlantic Ocean. They then move eastwards towards Europe. The southern

part of a depression contains the *warm sector*, which looks rather like the slice taken out of a cake. The rest of the depression contains colder air. The arrival of warm air is marked by a *warm front* while cold air follows the *cold front*. The fronts angle up from the ground on both sides of the warm sector. This is because warm air rises over colder air masses. The fronts and warm sector of a depression (Fig. 25) make up a distinctive pattern of pressure, wind directions, temperatures and clouds. Though no two depressions are the same, this general pattern is often repeated – a useful aid to forecasting.

---

12 Figure 25 shows the features of a depression. Using your knowledge of wind directions (p. 89) and cloud types (p. 91), complete the table below Fig. 25.

When a depression of this type moves across the British Isles you would first see the signs that are listed in column 3. Cirrus clouds ('mares' tails') and falling pressure suggest that bad weather is on the way. Where the warm front nears the ground (at B on Fig. 25), precipitation may continue for some time. At the cold front cumulonimbus clouds often give short-lived but very heavy showers. Between these

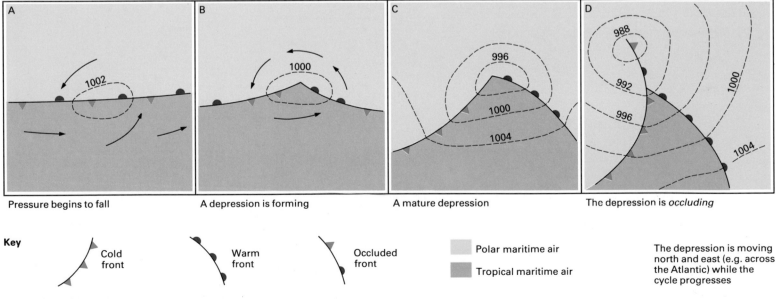

Key

Cold front

Warm front

Occluded front

Polar maritime air

Tropical maritime air

The depression is moving north and east (e.g. across the Atlantic) while the cycle progresses

A — Pressure begins to fall
B — A depression is forming
C — A mature depression
D — The depression is *occluding*

Fig. 24 The life cycle of an 'ideal' depression

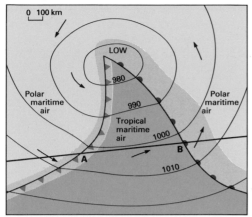

The cross-section follows the line marked across the map. Both use the same horizontal scale. Shading shows major rainfall areas.

periods of rain the warm sector is likely to have low cloud with drizzle or else clearer weather with scattered showers.

The sequence of events from the warning 'mare's tails' to the clearing showers after a cold front may take a very short time if the fronts are close together or when the depression is moving fast. Much of the forecaster's skill lies in deciding which part of the depression will cross the British Isles and whether it will pass straight over or linger, blocked by an anticyclone over Europe. If a depression is not being blocked it will probably move eastwards at about 60 km per hour.

As a depression travels towards Europe the cold front catches up with the warm front, lifting the warm sector off the ground (Fig. 26, p. 96). An *occluded front* on a weather map shows where this has happened. But even as one depression is dying or moving away from Britain, another is likely to come in from the Atlantic. There is often only a short spell of good weather associated with a ridge of high pressure between two depressions. Britain

Fig. 25 Map and block diagram of an 'ideal' depression

Metres
10 000

Depression moves east

Cirrus

Cumulo-nimbus

Stage 5   Stage 4   Stage 3   Stage 2   Stage 1

Warm air

5000

Cold front   Cumulus   Stratus   Alto-stratus

Cold air   Warm front

Warm sector   Nimbo-stratus   Cold air

Showers

Rain   Showers or drizzle

Heavy rain   Rain

A   B

0

500   1000   1500   2000

Note: The vertical scale is much larger than the horizontal scale.

	Column 1	Column 2	Column 3
	West of the cold front	In the warm sector	East of the warm front
AIR MASS: name, temperature (warm/cold)			
AIR PRESSURE (rising/steady/falling)			
WIND DIRECTION			
	Along the cold front	In the warm sector	Along the warm front
CLOUD TYPE(S)			
PRECIPITATION			

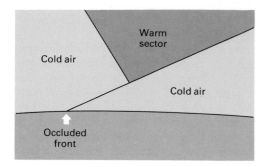

Fig. 26 Cross-section through an occluded depression

is only free from this sequence of depressions and short periods of fine weather when the country is dominated by an anticyclone.

13 Cut out a series of newspaper weather maps and follow the development, growth and death of a series of depressions. Pay particular attention to the routes they take and the weather in your home area as they pass.

14 Try your hand at weather forecasting. Copy the isobars, fronts, shading and numbering from Fig. 27 onto a piece of tracing paper. Copy the outline of Britain and western Europe onto white paper. Place the tracing paper (which represents the weather) over the white paper (which represents the ground). Now you can move the depression in the direction and at the speed expected by the forecasters.

'The depression is expected to cross Britain from west to east so that an imaginary line running through points A–D passes over Cardiff. It is January. A will reach Cardiff at 3 pm, B will arrive at 10 pm, C at 9 am the next day, and D at 2 pm.'

Give a weather forecast for Cardiff over this 24-hour period.

Anticyclones

Depressions pass over the British Isles in a matter of hours or a few days, but anticyclones are more slow-moving. We do not experience them very often but, once established, they are likely to stay for days

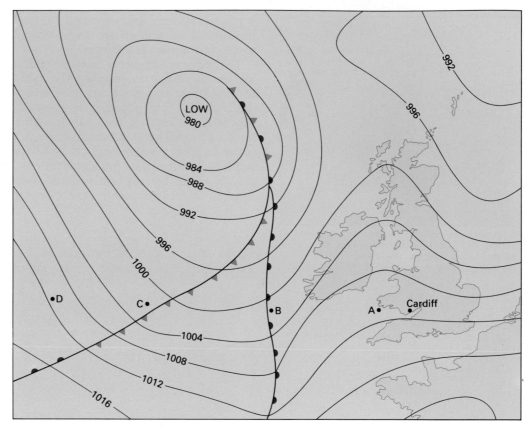

Fig. 27 Weather map for 2.00 pm on 18 January

or even weeks. Their gentle pressure gradients bring light winds and in summer their clear skies result in our hottest weather. In spring and autumn there may be heavy dew and some radiation fog at night, while in the winter the fog may last through the day or just lift a little to form stratus cloud. The simple barometer dial which suggests that high pressure automatically means fine weather is a little misleading in winter – but it is a fact that there is seldom any rainfall when an anticyclone is around.

Understanding depressions and anticyclones helps us to produce simple weather forecasts, but we should not be disappointed if we are sometimes caught out. Depressions change from day to day. One that seems to be *filling* and disappearing may suddenly *deepen* and become more active. One that seems to be passing straight across the British Isles may halt for 24 hours or even be pushed back into the Atlantic. The weather may

also show local variations. A forecast for the British Isles may predict clear skies and gentle winds and be generally correct. But at the same time, coastal areas may be foggy, some mountainous areas may have up-valley winds, and particularly hot inland regions may experience isolated convectional showers. The most accurate weather forecasts are those produced for local regions. Walkers wanting to know cloud conditions in the Lake District, or windsurfers interested in wind speeds along the Cornish coast, for example, can find this information by telephoning a specially recorded weather forecast for their area.

Fig. 28 is a satellite image of Northern Europe taken on 6th August 1987. Look at the pattern of clouds, which are shown in white and grey. A depression is moving over the British Isles and great swirls of cloud have formed along weather fronts. You can see that lines of clouds follow the

tion than a simple photograph. Unlike human eyes, satellite sensors can detect radiation from the earth both in the visible spectrum (which is what our eyes see) and also beyond, in the infra-red spectrum. As well as recording the clouds they can be used to discover the temperature of land, sea, or clouds and even to work out how much water vapour there is in the atmosphere. They are an impressive aid to weather forecasting.

Fig. 28 A satellite photograph of a depression crossing Britain

winds that are circulating anticlockwise around the depression. A cold front extends from North-West Spain to Brittany and then over central England. Clouds along the warm front cover most of the North Sea from Norway to Scotland. Over Ireland and the North Atlantic an occluded front leads to the centre of the depression. The mainland of Western Europe, which is an area of high pressure, is almost free of clouds.

Satellite photographs such as this are frequently used in television weather forecasts because they give a picture of the clouds that is easy to understand. But satellites actually give us far more informa-

World climates

We have seen that London and Armagh have different patterns of weather. London has less rain, colder winters and warmer summers. The two places have different *climates*.

Climates vary a great deal from place to place. We have seen the contrasts between north and south, east and west in a small area such as the British Isles. There are even local differences between mountains and valleys, towns and countryside. The same is true throughout the world, so there are many different climates. Fortunately, large areas have enough in common for us to divide the world into *climatic regions*. We could use just three regions – those with high temperatures (from the equator to 35° North and South), medium temperatures (from 35° to 70° North and South), and low temperatures (from 70° to the poles). These areas are called the *tropical*, *temperate* and *polar* zones. Temperatures do not suddenly change at latitudes 35° and 70°, but these are convenient dividing lines.

Figure 29 shows the world divided into climatic regions. Instead of the three simple temperature zones (tropical, temperate, polar), it shows 6 types of climate, which are based on rainfall as well as temperature. To understand the variations from one place to another, we must remember the influence of latitude that we studied on p. 86. This makes the north of Scotland colder than the south of England, but has much more effect if we compare temperatures at the north and south poles with the heat of the equator. Other factors that we need to understand are:

- the direction of the earth's major wind systems
- the distribution of land and sea, and the presence of warm or cool ocean currents
- the location of mountains and lowlands.

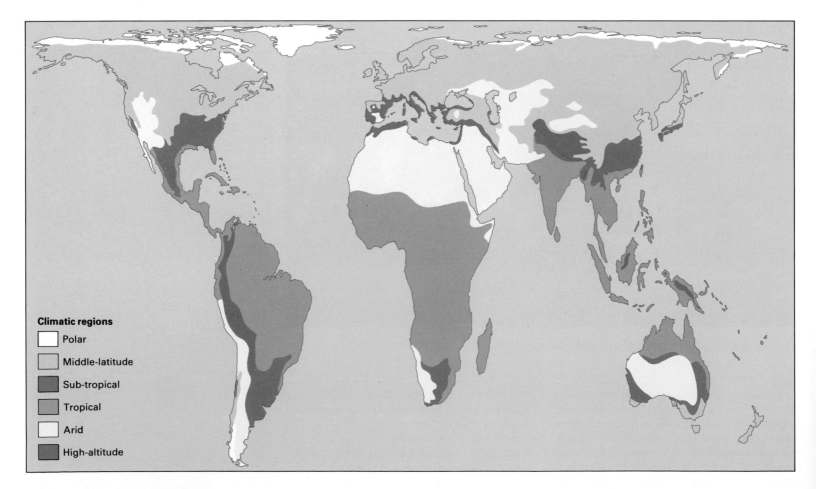

Climatic regions

- ☐ Polar
- ☐ Middle-latitude
- ☐ Sub-tropical
- ☐ Tropical
- ☐ Arid
- ☐ High-altitude

Fig. 29 The world's climatic regions

The general circulation

This is the name given to the overall pattern of air movements in the atmosphere. Areas near the equator receive vast amounts of energy from the sun. The heat causes huge convection currents of rising air, and there is generally a low-pressure area around the equator. Winds blow into this low-pressure area from the north and the south. They are diverted to the right in the northern hemisphere and to the left in the southern hemisphere, producing the north-east and south-east *trade winds*. The north-east trade winds are shown in Fig. 30.

What happens to the rising air at the equator? After rising it moves polewards and gently sinks towards the earth at about latitude 30° North and South. This results in the subtropical high-pressure areas. When this air reaches the ground, some moves into the depressions of temperate latitudes. The rest returns towards the equator as the trade winds.

In each hemisphere, therefore, there is an immense convection current (called the *Hadley Cell* after the meteorologist who discovered them). At ground level, the trade winds blow from an area of high pressure (subtropical high pressure) to an area of low pressure. At the equator the winds from the southern and northern hemispheres meet at the *inter-tropical convergence zone* (ITCZ).

---

15 Clouds and rain are usually caused by rising air. If air sinks towards the earth, clouds and rain are very unlikely. So would you expect the area of the ITCZ to be an area of dry or wet weather? What about the subtropical high-pressure area?

We have seen that some air from the subtropical high-pressure zone moves polewards into temperate latitudes. Here, together with colder air from polar regions, it is drawn into depressions.

The *prevailing* winds in temperate latitudes are westerlies, so west coasts generally have onshore winds. But these winds are more variable in direction than

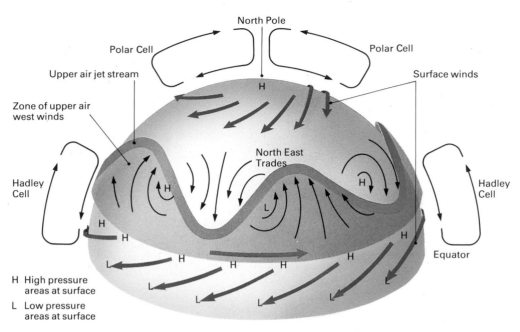

Fig. 30 The general circulation in the northern hemisphere

the trade winds. This is because they circle around the anticyclones and depressions that are typical of temperate areas. These pressure systems are linked to the jet-stream (see p. 88).

Where prevailing winds blow from the sea to the land they usually result in a rainy climate. Britain, with its prevailing south-west winds, is a good example of this. But if the prevailing winds have to cross a large area of continent they are likely to become very dry.

Land and sea

Look back to p. 85. Why does land tend to be hot in the summer and cold in the winter, whereas the sea shows smaller temperature variations? This has an important effect on climates. Near the coast, especially where prevailing winds blow from the sea, summers are warm rather than hot, and winters are mild rather than cold. In central continental areas there are much larger extremes of temperature. These different types of climate are known as *maritime* and *continental* types. As we have seen, they have different amounts of rainfall, as well as different temperature ranges.

Ocean currents are large, slowly moving bodies of water that can be identified by their temperature. When water moves from the equator into cooler areas, it is warmer than the rest of the ocean in those latitudes. It is therefore called a *warm current*. If water moves from cold areas towards the equator, it becomes a *cold current*.

The pattern of ocean currents is largely the result of prevailing winds. Figure 31 shows that where south-westerly winds cross the North Atlantic and North Pacific there are warm south-westerly currents.

The cold currents off the coasts of North and South America and off the African coast reflect the direction of the trade winds. In the southern hemisphere, the West Wind Drift in the ocean results from the westerly winds that blow around the world in these latitudes. The pattern is complicated by the continents which 'get in the way' of the ocean currents, as well as by differences in the temperatures and even the salinity (saltiness) of the ocean waters.

Ocean currents affect the temperature and the rainfall of nearby coastlines. Penzance in Cornwall is at the same latitude as

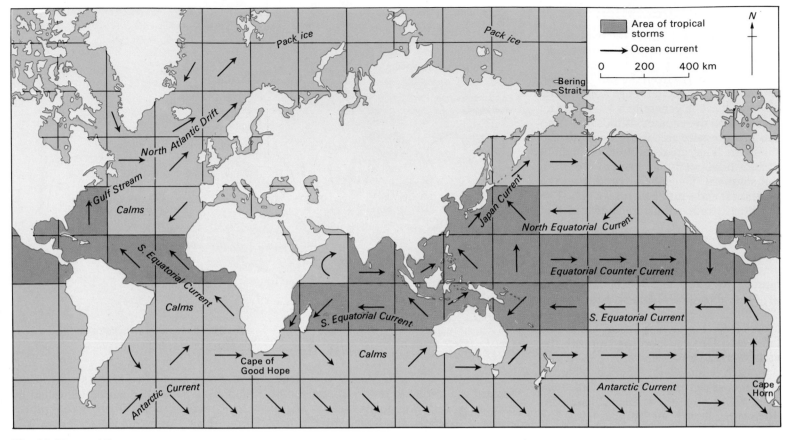

Fig. 31 The world's ocean currents

Newfoundland in eastern Canada, but its January temperature is 10°C warmer – the British Isles benefit from the warm waters of the North Atlantic Drift.

Rainfall is affected too because winds blowing over a cold current carry less moisture. That is one reason why even the coastal areas of the Sahara, Atacama, and Namib deserts are so dry.

Mountains and lowlands

Mountains are generally colder, wetter and windier than surrounding lowlands. They are colder because in the lower part of the atmosphere, temperatures decrease with height. The sun heats the earth and in turn the earth heats the lower layers of the atmosphere. Mountains are affected by winds blowing in the higher, colder air.

These winds, high above the earth, are not slowed down by friction with the earth's surface, so mountain areas experience strong winds, especially when they are funnelled along valleys. The high rainfall (or snowfall) of mountains results from air rising over the mountain barrier and cooling to dew-point.

Areas downwind of mountain barriers have a much lower rainfall. The Prairies east of the Rocky Mountains, and the Vale of York east of the Pennines, both show this rainshadow effect.

These influences explain the pattern of world climates shown in Fig. 29. We will now look at two of these climates in more detail.

Desert climate

16 Look at the desert areas on Fig. 29.
 a What is the average latitude (north and south) for deserts (not including the Gobi and Patagonian deserts)?
 b On which side of continents (east or west) are most deserts found?

Deserts occupy about 20% of the world's land surface. The exact percentage depends on the definition of 'deserts'. As a rough guide, they are areas with less than 250 mm of rain a year. In the tropics deserts may have more rain than this, but much of it evaporates in the high temperatures.

Most deserts are in the zone of subtropical high pressure. Though the ground becomes very hot, only small convection currents can build up because this is an area of descending air. The convection currents seldom rise high enough for clouds to form. Occasionally, however, the convection overcomes the gently descending air and heavy showers follow. Desert rainfall is very unpredictable and in one year there may be as much rain as in the last ten or twenty put together.

The prevailing winds in most desert areas are the north-east and south-east trades. These become increasingly dry as they blow across the land, so deserts tend to be on the western side of continents. Sometimes this effect is even greater because the desert lies in a rainshadow.

---

17 Use an atlas to find out the names of the mountain ranges which prevent much rain reaching
  a the Atacama Desert
  b southern California
  c the Gobi Desert.

Deserts sometimes extend right up to the coast, which may seem surprising. Surely winds from the sea would bring rain? But this is where a special factor comes into play. The oceans near tropical deserts contain cold water which rises to the surface from great depths, or moves in from lower latitudes (Fig. 31). Any winds blowing from the west will therefore be cool and unable to bring much moisture to the land.

---

18 Name the cold current off **a** the Atacama Desert **b** the Namib Desert.

We have seen that a desert is defined as an arid (dry) area. It is not necessarily hot. It is true that the highest shade temperature ever recorded was 58°C in the Sahara Desert, but night temperatures can be low. During the day the sun beats down from a cloudless sky but at night heat can easily escape by radiation. The ground may cool sufficiently for dew to form and this has been known to save the lives of desert travellers who would otherwise have died of thirst. Deserts have the largest diurnal (daily) temperature ranges in the world.

Mediterranean climate

Areas with a Mediterranean climate, which is sometimes described as *warm temperate maritime*, have most of their rain in the winter, and a summer drought. The mildness of the winters and the heat and sunshine of the summers have encouraged the growth of tourism in many such areas.

---

19 a Use Fig. 29 and an atlas to find the names of four areas outside Europe that have a Mediterranean climate.
  b What do you notice about (i) the latitude of Mediterranean climates (ii) on which side of continents they are found?
  c Plot a climate graph (similar to Fig. 23) for the data shown in Fig. 32. Remember to use a bar chart for the rainfall and a line graph for the temperature.
  d What are the main differences between the climates of London and Palermo?

The mildness and dampness of the winters are associated with the prevailing westerly winds of this season. These winds bring in the stored-up warmth of the ocean. From May to August the sun is overhead in the northern hemisphere, so all the pressure systems shown in Fig. 30 move north. This means that countries around the Mediterranean Sea frequently experience the high pressure that is common throughout the year in the Sahara Desert. This guarantees many hours of dry, sunny weather.

---

20 Mountainous areas in the Mediterranean countries have a colder climate than the surrounding lowlands. Name
  a a mountain range in southern Spain
  b the mountains in northern Morocco that rise to heights of over 3000 m.

Month	Average monthly temperature (°C)	Average monthly rainfall (mm)
J	11	70
F	12	40
M	13	50
A	15	50
M	18	20
J	22	10
J	25	0
A	26	20
S	23	40
O	20	75
N	17	65
D	13	55

Fig. 32 Temperature and rainfall figures for Palermo, Sicily, Italy

9 | Soils

Warning: *You should not handle soils if there are cuts on your hands, because of the risk of infection.*

Figure 1 shows how important the soil is to farmers like Jim Martin. If it is blown away, his crop of wheat cannot grow. The soil provides a huge store of moisture and food (*nutrients*) which plants use for their growth. The nutrients are returned to the soil when leaves fall to the ground or plants die. The soil contains most of the small creatures that break down dead material and prepare it for further use by plants.

1 Write out the following sentences, completing them with information from Fig. 1:

The soil that is blown away from wheat farms in Kansas is very dry and dusty. Jim Martin described it as 'like _____ _____'. Erosion is most likely to happen when the weather has been _____ and when the wind is _____.

2 List four methods used in Kansas to reduce wind erosion.

What is soil?

There is a difference between sand on a beach, and a sandy soil. The clay used for brick-making is a rock and is not quite the same as a clay soil. In each case the soil contains an extra ingredient, the vegetation that has rotted and broken down to

Big Dust

Every year, Jim Martin, aged 50, does battle with seasonal wind erosion, staving off a re-run of the calamitous Kansas Dust Bowl of the 1930s. This spring he is closer to losing than ever. So far, he estimates, 80 per cent of his land at Solomon, 20 miles west of Abilene, has been "blown out" and 30 per cent of his crop is beyond recovery.

March 14 will go down as a day of infamy in local annals, the day the state saw the worst dust storm since 1937. In the Big Dust, the afternoon sun was blacked out by columns of dust as fine and grey as gunpowder, reaching 10,000ft into the sky.

Since then, it has swirled and settled, stripping soil from the roots of seedling winter wheat in one field, burying the struggling plants in another.

About 520,000 acres have so far been damaged by dust storms - technically wind erosion - in Kansas. The Department of Agriculture in Washington estimates that 4.7 million acres have been damaged throughout the Great Plains.

After last summer's record drought, this is an indicator that the winter has done little to relieve conditions. Only spring rains and snow-melt from the Rocky Mountains can alleviate the prospect of another summer drought; the land is in poor condition for a second onslaught.

"We went into the wind erosion season with poor cover in much of the Great Plains because of the drought," says Winston Scaling, head of the Agriculture Department's Soil Conservation Service. "Then, this winter, we have had a combination of no snow cover and high winds in many areas."

Martin and his fellow farmers reacted quickly to the dust storms. They would sacrifice the crop to save the land.

This involved ploughing over seedlings with a chisel plough, consisting of rows of steel prongs designed to create ridges about six inches tall. The rapid freezing and thawing of the Plains leaves the surface soil dry and dusty - "like talcum powder," said Martin - and turning up heavier soil creates miniature windbreaks over the surface of the fields.

At 62, Tom Roberts of the Wheat Quality Council has his own bitter memories of the Dirty Thirties in Kansas. In despair, his father abandoned farm and family, leaving his wife and four children on a 32-acre farm. The dust left Roberts with an allergic cough. It has been playing up of late. "We won't go back to those days - we learnt too much and haven't forgotten it, " he said.

He pointed to hedgerows, extensively planted by teams of the unemployed in a welfare project at the height of the 1930 Dust Bowl; to the stubble now routinely left in the fields to provide cover; and to the regular rotation that leaves half the land fallow with grass. Clusters of oak, sycamore and prairie pine have been left in hollows, resented by farmers for the moisture they absorb, but welcomed in a "dirty" year.

Fig. 1 Extract from the *Daily Telegraph*, 31 March 1989

form *humus*. It is humus that gives most British soils their brownish colour.

A handful of soil contains some living matter such as plant roots, earthworms and bacteria, but it mainly consists of broken-down rock particles chemically combined with humus. The rock particles have

usually been formed by the *weathering* of the solid rock which lies beneath. Between these particles are gaps containing air and water.

Two of the main factors that influence the type of soil are, therefore, the sort of rock from which it is formed, and the amount and type of humus it contains. Other influences are shown in Fig. 2. You will see that one of these is *time*. Thousands of years are needed for a deep, rich soil to form. In many upland areas of Britain the soil was carried away by glaciers in the last Ice Age, and these regions still have thin soils, 10 000 years or more later. This is a warning to all who cultivate the land. If we allow soils to be blown or washed away, our descendants will suffer for many generations.

3 Study Fig. 2 and think about each of these influences on soils:

a *Slope*. Would you expect to find thick soils at the bottom of a steep slope or higher up? Why?

b *Rock type*. Would you expect to find thick soils in an area of hard rock or in an area of soft rock? Why?

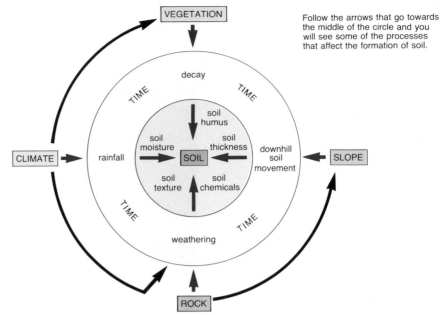

Follow the arrows that go towards the middle of the circle and you will see some of the processes that affect the formation of soil.

Fig. 2 Factors affecting soil formation

Soil description

Soils vary from one place to another. They may be thin or deep, fertile or infertile, damp or well drained. They can be looked at from several points of view.

Texture

Studying soil texture **P**

1 Take a small handful of soil, wet it (use spit if necessary!) and squeeze it until there is no surplus moisture.

2 Try to make your soil into each of the following shapes, starting at '1 Cone' and seeing how far you can get towards '5 Smooth bent worm'. The final shape you can manage to make tells you which soil texture you have.

Shape	Type of soil	
1 Cone	Sand	(coarse)
2 Ball	Loamy sand	
3 Straight worm	Loam	
4 Bent worm which cracks	Clayey loam or loamy clay	
5 Smooth bent worm	Clay	(fine)

If you can make all five shapes, you have a clay. If you can only make the first two, you have a loamy sand.

Now wash your hands!

Studying the proportion of sand, silt, and clay particles in soil **P**

1 Take a handful of dry soil and gently break it into a powder. Remove roots and other vegetable matter.

2 Place about 2 cm of soil in the bottom of a jam jar, add water nearly to the top, and stir or shake.

3 Sand particles will sink to the bottom almost immediately whereas silt particles will take a few hours, and clay particles a day or more. You should be able to distinguish layers as the soil settles to the bottom of the glass.

4 Repeat with soil samples taken from different places and compare the proportions of sand, silt, and clay.

These exercises are simple tests which you can carry out to see whether a soil consists mainly of fine particles (*clay*), coarse particles (*sand*), or whether it is a *loam*, made up of a mixture of clay, sand, and *silt* (medium-sized) particles.

The soil's texture has a strong influence on the amount of water and plant nutrients it holds. Because clay consists of small particles fitting closely together, the *pores* (gaps between the particles) are small. Water which enters the pores is held by *surface tension* and has difficulty in draining away. So a clay soil is often damp and poorly drained.

Water moves downwards more easily in a sandy soil, which therefore dries out quickly. In some ways this is an advantage, but unfortunately the water moving through the soil takes away many of the plant nutrients, leaving the topsoil infertile. For this reason sandy soils need frequent doses of fertiliser and are known as *hungry* soils. Loams are usually well drained but not too hungry, and therefore give some of the most fertile farmland.

Structure

The individual soil particles are attached to each other and build up larger soil structures called *peds* (Fig. 3). Cracks between peds are important for the movement of air and water. If these structures are damaged by heavy machinery, the natural drainage is less effective and the soil may become waterlogged.

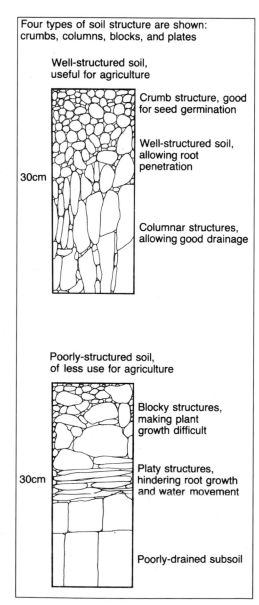

Four types of soil structure are shown: crumbs, columns, blocks, and plates

Well-structured soil, useful for agriculture

30cm

Crumb structure, good for seed germination

Well-structured soil, allowing root penetration

Columnar structures, allowing good drainage

Poorly-structured soil, of less use for agriculture

30cm

Blocky structures, making plant growth difficult

Platy structures, hindering root growth and water movement

Poorly-drained subsoil

Fig. 3 Soil peds

Fig. 4 Peat cutting in Ireland. The slabs of peat will be stacked, left to dry, and then used as fuel. Peat soils in lowland areas are fertile if drained because they contain plenty of decayed vegetation

Moisture

The amount of water held in the soil is influenced by its texture, and also by the underlying rock type, the amount of rainfall, and the slope of the land. If the underlying rock is *impermeable* – that is, it does not allow water to drain away – the soil will become damp. In extreme cases it can become waterlogged and little will grow except for moss. This eventually decays to give thick layers of *peat* (Fig. 4). Wet soils are also found on flat land where water does not drain away easily, in valley bottoms, and in mountainous areas with high rainfall.

People can alter the moisture content of soil by drainage or irrigation. Poor cultivation methods also affect soil moisture. If a field is ploughed when it is very damp, the ploughshare *smears* the particles together, forming an impermeable layer. Another effect, known as *poaching*, occurs when tractors or cattle press down on damp soil and compress it so that little rainwater can sink in. The same effect is sometimes seen around the goal mouth of a soccer pitch.

Studying the moisture content of soil P

Using a small moisture meter:

- Compare the moisture content of the upper and lower parts of a flowerbed or a natural slope.
- Compare the moisture content of plant pots containing sandy soil, clay soil, and peat.
- Carry out your experiment a few hours after rain has fallen or the soil has been watered.

Soil chemistry

Farmers and gardeners add many fertilisers to the soil. Whether they use animal manure or artificial fertiliser, the main aim is to change the chemical composition of

Investigating soil pH

1 Use an electronic pH meter or a chemical soil test kit to investigate the pH of soils in your local area. The diagram below shows you how to set about this. You will find the colours in the diagram if you carry out a chemical pH test.

2 Try to explain any variations you find. For example, a geological map may show changes of rock type from place to place.

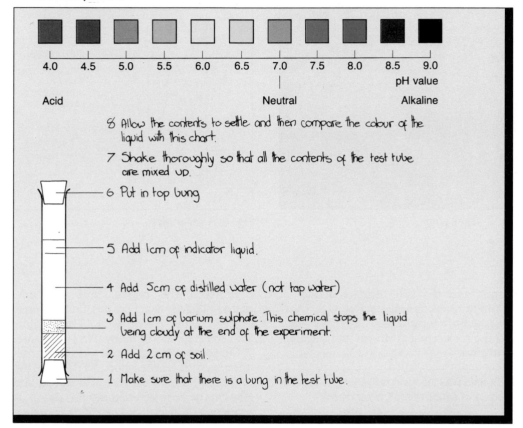

| 4.0 | 4.5 | 5.0 | 5.5 | 6.0 | 6.5 | 7.0 | 7.5 | 8.0 | 8.5 | 9.0 |

pH value

Acid   Neutral   Alkaline

8 Allow the contents to settle and then compare the colour of the liquid with this chart.

7 Shake thoroughly so that all the contents of the test tube are mixed up.

6 Put in top bung

5 Add 1cm of indicator liquid.

4 Add 5cm of distilled water (not tap water)

3 Add 1cm of barium sulphate. This chemical stops the liquid being cloudy at the end of the experiment.

2 Add 2 cm of soil.

1 Make sure that there is a bung in the test tube.

the soil in order to improve plant growth.

Soils that contain large amounts of lime because they have developed on limestone or chalk are generally *alkaline*, whereas those on granite tend to be *acid*. The acidity of a soil is measured on the *pH scale*.

Plants rely on many different chemicals for healthy growth, and these have to be replaced if they are in short supply. Natural farmyard manure returns nitrogen, potassium and phosphorus to the soil, and these are also the usual contents of artificial fertilisers. Manure has the added benefit of maintaining the humus content of the soil.

4 Read the extract from the *Farmer's Weekly* (Fig. 5). What pH is regarded as harmful to many crops? How are farmers advised to correct the soil acidity? Try to explain how the treatment works.

5 Adding chemical fertilisers to the soil may increase crop yields but it can have harmful side-effects. Study Fig. 5 and list the problems that may result from the use of large quantities of fertiliser.

BEWARE OF HIGH ACIDITY

Farmers are taking enormous risks by letting soil acidity increase.

*ADAS surveys of nearly 4000 fields show 12% of arable fields have pHs lower than 6.0. Many crops, in particular barley and sugar beet, are affected at a pH of 5.9 and growers should be aware of letting their fields fall to such low values.

ADAS soil scientist Dick Skinner advises those with field averages of 6.5 or below to check for localised patches that could be even worse. With detailed sampling, lime deficient areas can be treated with more lime and those that require none can be bypassed.

Growers can pick out these areas using pH indicator kits and, if care is taken, these can back up independent or commercial company tests.

If lime is applied exactly where it is needed in-field variations can be reduced and more uniform crops grown.

*ADAS : Agricultural Development and Advisory Service.

Fig. 5 Extract from the *Farmer's Weekly*

Colour

The colour of soil is influenced by chemicals present in the soil. Most British soils are brown near the surface, though lower down they may be very light in colour, or even bluish-green (see Fig. 9 on p. 107).

Soil colour should be recorded carefully using a colour chart. Some shades are given in Fig. 6, or you could make up your own chart from the small cards of paint colour samples available in DIY shops.

Recording soil colour

Use a chart like the one in Fig. 6 to record the colour of soils taken from different places. If the soils do not show great variations in colour you may need to make a chart that has more shades of brown. This will help you to record small differences between soils.

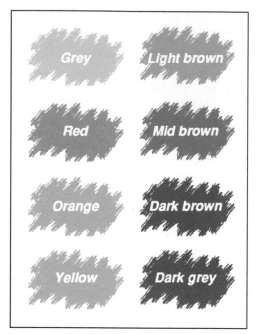

Fig. 6 A soil colour chart

Fig. 7 A soil auger

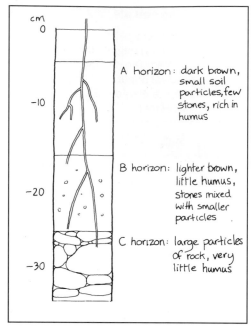

Fig. 8 A soil profile

Soil profiles

So far we have examined the surface layers of the soil. But it is just as important to know what soils are like lower down. After all, that is where the plant roots obtain moisture and nutrients. A thorough investigation involves the digging of soil pits, but for most purposes a soil auger can provide all the information you need. It can be used for finding the depth of the soil as well as for looking at the various layers or *horizons* that make up a *soil profile*.

Let us examine a typical woodland soil. Below last year's *litter* (dead leaves) there will be a layer of leaves which have decomposed to form humus. Beneath this lies the *A horizon* where humus is mixed with small particles of weathered rock. Water drains through this horizon, dissolving some of the chemicals and carrying them downwards. This process is known as *leaching* and in areas of high rainfall or sandy soils most of the nutrients are washed out of the A horizon.

These dissolved chemicals are washed down into the *B horizon*. Here there is little

humus and the soil consists mainly of weathered rock fragments. Below, in the *C horizon*, little weathering has taken place and the rock remains almost in its original condition.

---

6 Explain why leaching is likely to be rapid in areas of **a** high rainfall, **b** sandy soil.

The behaviour of water in the soil is one of the main reasons why British soils vary from place to place. The *podzol* (Fig. 9) occurs where there is strong leaching. Humus and iron are removed from the A horizon, leaving it light in colour and infertile. The B horizon is likely to be darker, for this is where the iron and other minerals are deposited. These sometimes form a distinct layer known as an *ironpan*.

At the other extreme, on damp clays and on low-lying ground, pores between the soil particles are filled with water rather than air. Iron in the soil has a greenish or bluish tinge in waterlogged areas, but along cracks and roots where air can penetrate it is brown or red. These waterlogged soils are known as *gleys*.

Between the podzol and the gley, neither heavily leached nor badly waterlogged, is the *brown earth*. This slightly acid soil is typical of many parts of Britain.

On some slopes the soils form a clear sequence, with leached podzols near the top of the hill, brown earths lower down, and gleys at the base where the soil is damp. A sequence such as this is called a *soil catena*.

Certain rock types also give distinctive soil profiles. When limestone is weathered, for instance, most of the resulting material is dissolved, so there are few particles to form a B horizon. *Rendzina* soils on chalk and limestone therefore have a thin A horizon which passes straight to a C horizon (Fig. 9).

---

7 a Use Fig. 9 to write a short description of a brown earth soil.

b See if you can discover, either from fieldwork or from published soil maps, whether any of the soils shown in Fig. 9 occur in your home area.

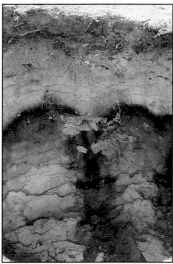

▼ **Podzol** The upper layer is grey because the iron is leached out. The brown colour lower down shows where the iron is deposited

◀ **Gley** There is air in the upper, brown layers of soil. Lower down, where the soil is waterlogged, the colour changes to grey-blue

◀ **Rendzina** Notice how thin the soil layer is. It contains pieces of weathered chalk that have not yet been completely dissolved

◀ **Brown Earth** This has not been leached as much as the podzol so the top layer is brown rather than grey. Think about where the changes of *horizon* occur

Fig. 9 Soil profiles

Studying soil profiles　P

1　Use a soil auger (or a spade if you have permission to dig a pit) to obtain a series of samples down through the soil. Make a note of changes in colour and texture at different levels. Can you identify any soil horizons?

2　You can make a record of different soil profiles by drawing a column 5 cm wide down the middle of a piece of paper. Mark a scale along the column so as to scale the entire depth of soil onto this one page. If you have identified different horizons, show these on your column.

3　Crush small samples of soil taken from various depths to a powder, and use a wet finger to 'paint' soil onto the column at the correct depths. Add notes about texture, pH and humus alongside the column.

Soil and the farmer

Soil is one of the earth's most precious resources, and many people are concerned that it is being damaged by modern farming methods. There are a number of problems that may result when people try to increase agricultural production.

FARMLAND THREATENED BY WATER

Nearly half of all arable land in Britain is being threatened by erosion, a report by the Soil Association claims.

But wind-borne erosion, in the form of "dust storms", encouraged by the removal of hedges and other windbreaks, is confined to only a few areas, and is insignificant compared to the effects of water, it says.

Until recently, water-induced erosion was not thought to be a serious problem in Britain. But in the past three or four decades the move towards more intensive agriculture, the abandonment of traditional mixed farming and crop rotation, have caused a significant deterioration.

Some reports have recorded losses of up to 200 tonnes a hectare a year. On relatively thin soils, such as the South Downs , productive capacity may be totally destroyed within a few decades.

It calls for an urgent, detailed assessment of the actual, and potential, extent of erosion.

Fig. 10 Extract from *The Times*

The Prairies

Despite the great natural fertility of the Prairies, mistakes and misfortune have resulted in problems for farmers both in the 1980s (Fig. 1) and in the 1930s.

8 a Locate the Prairies on Fig. 1, p. 102. Much of this area has fertile *chernozem* soils (Fig. 11). How do these differ from the brown earth soil typical of many parts of Britain?

b List the features of a chernozem soil that make it so fertile.

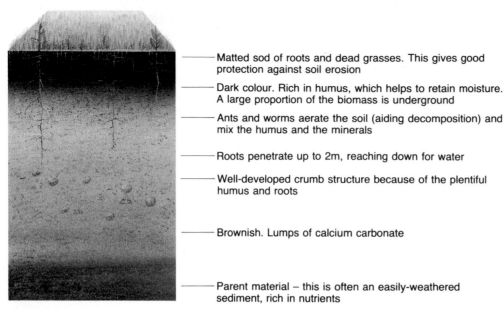

Matted sod of roots and dead grasses. This gives good protection against soil erosion

Dark colour. Rich in humus, which helps to retain moisture. A large proportion of the biomass is underground

Ants and worms aerate the soil (aiding decomposition) and mix the humus and the minerals

Roots penetrate up to 2m, reaching down for water

Well-developed crumb structure because of the plentiful humus and roots

Brownish. Lumps of calcium carbonate

Parent material – this is often an easily-weathered sediment, rich in nutrients

Fig. 11 Chernozem soil

In the 1930s, farmers growing wheat in the Mid-Western States of the USA suffered a series of dry years. The crops failed and the parched soil was left without any vegetation cover. Winds blowing over this almost treeless area removed millions of tonnes of soil. When the rain fell the soil was unprotected and millions of tonnes were removed by muddy torrents of water, forming gullies several metres deep.

Could this disaster have been avoided? The early colonists took the farming methods of western Europe to the drier conditions of the Prairies. The methods were unsuitable and should have been adapted to the different conditions. Many changes have now taken place. Some farmers have abandoned wheat and have converted their land to pasture, which gives the soil more protection. Others use *dry farming* techniques. Special ploughs cultivate the soil without turning it over. This reduces the loss of moisture from evaporation, as the damp soil is not exposed. *Contour ploughing* (ploughing along the slope rather than up and down hillsides) makes it more difficult for gullies to form. If soils are to be protected for the future, farmers in the Prairies have to show great respect for the power of the wind and the rain.

9 a How was the Dust Bowl of the 1930s created?

b Describe the dry farming techniques that help make modern farming more stable than that of the 1930s.

Irrigation

Adding extra water to the soil in dry parts of the world has done much to increase crop production. But if too much water is applied, minerals in the soil are dissolved. In a hot climate where there is rapid evaporation, water is drawn up to the soil surface, bringing the dissolved minerals with it. Here the water evaporates, leaving an infertile crust of salt and other minerals. If there is too little irrigation, the crops may fail; if there is too much, the soil may be ruined.

It is difficult for farmers to avoid this problem of salty soils unless drains are put into the soil allowing the salt to be carried away with any surplus water. But this is expensive and amounts of water have to be very carefully controlled. Serious damage has been done to the soil in places as far apart as California, Egypt, and Pakistan.

Clearing tropical forests

Looking at the Amazon rainforest with its tall trees and dense undergrowth, we might expect the soil below to be very fertile. Yet when large areas of woodland are cleared for cultivation, farmers are often disappointed with the crops they try to grow. Research has shown that the soil does not have a rich supply of nutrients.

The dense forest is a result of the rapid *nutrient cycle* (Fig. 12). Instead of remaining in the soil for a long time, the nutrients (plant food) are constantly being used. But when the trees are chopped down and burned, many of the nutrients disappear. Each time crops are grown and harvested, more nutrients are used up. Crop yields decline rapidly unless large amounts of fertiliser are used. Eventually the soil loses its structure and is easily eroded by the heavy tropical rainfall. This reminds us of the delicate balance existing in nature and of how careful we must be when we are making changes.

10 Study Fig. 12. Follow the cycle round once and write a description of what happens to the chemicals (nutrients) released by weathering below a tropical forest.

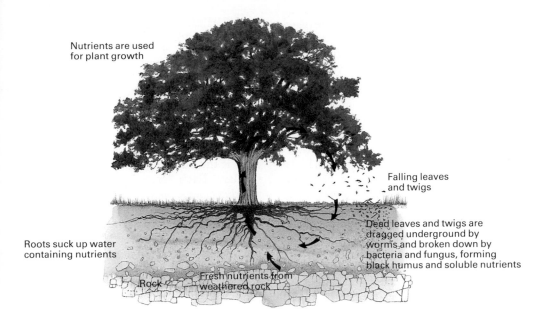

Nutrients are used for plant growth

Roots suck up water containing nutrients

Falling leaves and twigs

Dead leaves and twigs are dragged underground by worms and broken down by bacteria and fungus, forming black humus and soluble nutrients

Rock

Fresh nutrients from weathered rock

Fig. 12 The nutrient cycle – this is especially rapid in tropical rainforests, where leaf litter can be broken down in six weeks, compared with a year in a temperate forest

The wind can now sweep across the fields without obstruction, so soil erosion is even more likely.

- Modern artificial fertilisers improve soil chemistry but do not replace humus, unlike old-fashioned farmyard manure. This means that the soil particles do not bind together well, and are more easily eroded by the wind.
- In places, heavy modern tractors have damaged the soil structure. This can encourage erosion by both water and wind.

Most farmers are aware of these problems and are trying to reduce the risk of soil erosion. But a few, looking for short-term profits, may be causing long-term damage to the soil.

11 Write two short articles about the methods used by some Fenland farmers to increase their profits. The first article should argue the case from the farmers' point of view. The second article should be a criticism of these farming methods.

Conclusion

Ploughing, draining, irrigation, and the removal of nutrients by harvesting crops, can all damage the soil. But careful farming, based on modern research or well-tried tradition, and using crop rotation, suitable cultivation methods, and the replacement of essential humus and minerals, will maintain the soil for future generations. The danger is that rapid population growth results in the over-use of poor soils in a desperate effort to feed the hungry. In the long term this might spell disaster.

Fig. 13 The large open fields of the Fens

Case Study

The Fens of East Anglia

This low-lying land, once marshy, has now been drained to make a very fertile farming region. Unfortunately, several factors have led to soil erosion, sometimes even to dust storms, when large quantities of soil are whipped into the air and blown away:

- The peat and silt soils have dried out as a result of being drained, so they are now more easily eroded by the wind.
- Since the Second World War, many farmers have increased the size of their fields by removing trees and hedges.

10 | Vegetation

1 Draw a graph to show the number of plant species found on Krakatoa from 1883 to 1934. (Remember to plot your graph so that the years are accurately spaced along the horizontal axis.)

One way in which the earth differs from other planets is that much of its surface is covered by plants. But imagine a tropical island where there is nothing but bare rock. This was how the island of Krakatoa (near Java) looked in 1883 after all its plants and animals were destroyed in a huge volcanic eruption. Yet from this bleak start the vegetation recovered remarkably quickly:

Year	Total number of plant species	Typical plants
1883	0	All plants killed.
1886	26	Simple forms of plant life such as lichens and ferns.
1897	64	A thin soil had developed in many places. Woodland growing near the coast, grasses on the higher slopes.
1908	115	The woodland contained more species and was also found in inland valleys.
1934	271	Woodland covered the higher slopes as well as the valleys and coastal lowlands.

The work of scientists recording the number of plant species on Krakatoa has shown that vegetation can change over long periods of time. Similar changes have been noted in Britain, where a patch of abandoned land will soon be overgrown with grass and weeds. In 10 or 20 years there may be sizeable bushes and shrubs. In a hundred years trees will be growing and the land will be covered with something approaching the 'natural' vegetation. This series of changes is known as a *plant succession*. When the final stage in the succession has been reached, the area is occupied by *climax vegetation*.

The nature of the succession and the climax vegetation varies from place to place: compare the sparse, drought-resistant plants of deserts with the dense forests of tropical areas, or the oak woodlands of lowland Britain with the pines and spruces of Scandinavia. Climate is largely responsible for these variations. But there are other factors at work: different plants grow on chalky soils, in marshes, or on heaths, even if the climate in those three areas is similar. Each area has its own distinctive *plant community*.

The composition of a plant community can be explained by the factors shown in Fig. 1. These are divided for convenience into physical and biological factors, but there is a great deal of overlap. Fire is counted as a physical influence, but it can be started by people. Animals are biological but their presence is affected by physical influences such as rainfall and

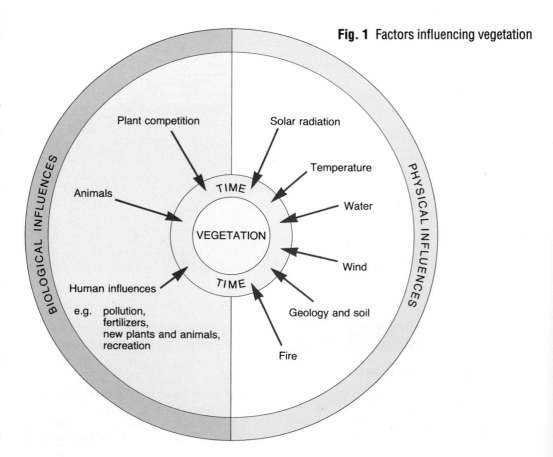

Fig. 1 Factors influencing vegetation

temperature. In fact, almost every factor shown affects every other factor in some way.

Notice that these factors require *time* in which to operate. Plant successions last tens, hundreds, or thousands of years. Plant evolution can be traced back to fossils of plants in rocks 2000 million years old, and the type of evolution has varied from place to place. For example, most trees in Australia are varieties of eucalyptus, but these were not found in other parts of the world until people introduced them to areas of Europe and Africa, where they have since grown very successfully.

Figure 2 shows the types of climax veg-

etation in different parts of the world. If you look back to Fig. 29 on p. 99 you will notice that these areas are strongly influenced by the types of climate. This is not the only influence, of course. In this chapter we look at five types of climax vegetation and see how they have also been affected by some of the other factors shown in Fig.1.

---

2 Compare Fig. 2 with Fig. 29 on p. 99. Name the vegetation and climate types in
a the British Isles
b Northern Canada
c Central Australia

Vegetation should always be understood together with its *environment* (surroundings). The soil, vegetation, climate, animals, and people in an area combine to make an *ecosystem*. Some ecosystems are more beautiful, more useful, or more fragile than others, but they are all important. An ecosystem can be defined as 'the plants and animals in an area, together with their surroundings'.

Fig. 2 The world's vegetation regions

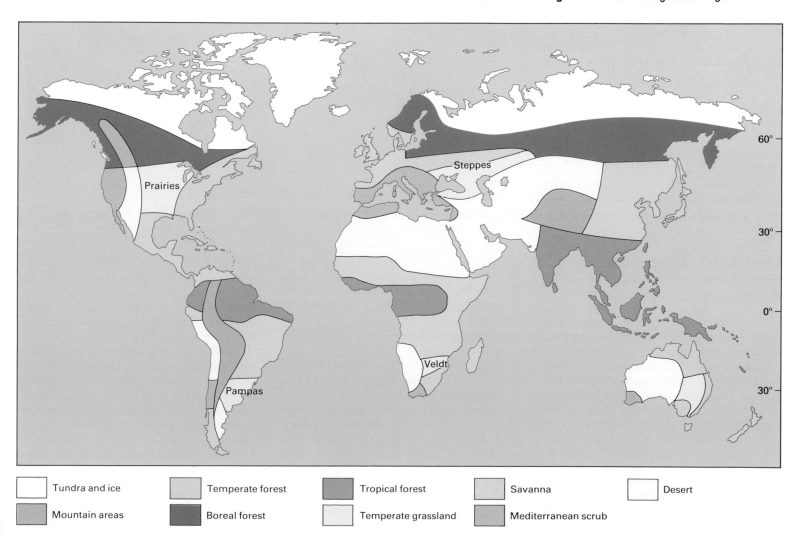

Tundra and ice

Mountain areas

Temperate forest

Boreal forest

Tropical forest

Temperate grassland

Savanna

Mediterranean scrub

Desert

111

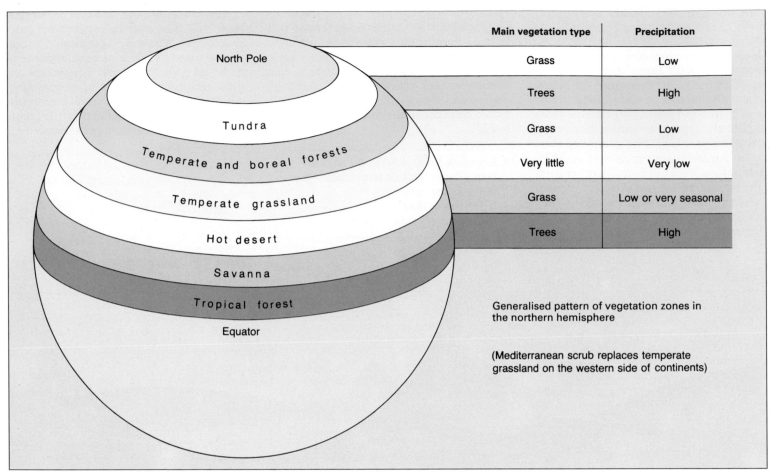

	Main vegetation type	Precipitation
North Pole	Grass	Low
	Trees	High
Tundra	Grass	Low
Temperate and boreal forests	Very little	Very low
Temperate grassland	Grass	Low or very seasonal
Hot desert	Trees	High
Savanna		
Tropical forest		
Equator		

Generalised pattern of vegetation zones in the northern hemisphere

(Mediterranean scrub replaces temperate grassland on the western side of continents)

Fig. 3 Vegetation regions around the world: a simplified version of Fig. 2 on p. 111, showing the vegetation regions as bands around the globe

Tropical rainforest

The forest environment

Tropical rainforest covers large areas where heavy rainfall occurs throughout the year. Temperatures are constantly high, averaging 25°C or more. Trees lose and replace their leaves gradually (they are *evergreen*) rather than shedding them for the winter like most British trees (*deciduous*). The vegetation never stops growing.

These forests are so dark at ground level that there is little undergrowth. Nor is there a thick layer of leaves and rotting vegetation underfoot. A leaf that would take years to rot in northern Europe will break down in only a couple of months in these hot, sticky conditions.

3 Study Fig. 2 and use an atlas to name five countries that have large areas of tropical forest.

The huge quantity of wood and leaves in tropical forests might suggest that the soil is very fertile, but appearances are often deceptive. At any one time most plant nutrients are within the vegetation rather than in the soil. When trees are felled and removed, the nutrients disappear with them. So a farmer moving into a newly cleared area could well find that crop yields rapidly decline. Traditional methods of *shifting cultivation* faced this problem by abandoning the land after a few years. If there is a large area of forest and only a small population, the farmer can move on to clear another patch of forest. But with rapid population growth this may no longer be possible.

There is a great variety of both plants and animals within a tropical evergreen forest. A hectare of woodland in Britain might contain five or six types of tree, whereas in the same area of Amazon rainforest there might be a hundred.

4 Most of the beef raised on cattle ranches in Central and South America is exported to the USA, mainly to make hamburgers for sale in fast-food restaurants and takeaways. An estimated 9m³ of forest is cleared for each hamburger! The price of

Epiphytes

Dense growth of moss

Lianas and stranglers

Buttress roots

Many different tree species. *Stands* of the same species are rare. This hinders commercial forestry

Epiphytes – small shrubs and herbs living in patches of soil or humus in the boughs of trees. Many orchids are epiphytes.

Lianas – woody, climbing plants.

Stranglers – begin life high in the trees. They send roots down into the soil and may eventually strangle the host tree.

Litter – fallen leaves in the early stages of rotting.

Termites – ant-like creatures which play an important part in the recycling of nutrients as they break down woody tissues.

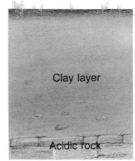

Clay layer

Acidic rock

THE LAYERED FOREST

'Emergent' species. The top of the forest is windy, so leaves are narrow to reduce transpiration. Seeds and pollen are dispersed by the wind. The trees have broad crowns.

Main canopy layer. Leaves are angled to catch as much sunlight as possible, and have 'drip tips' to shed rainwater. Pollen is carried by birds and insects, which are attracted by colourful flowers. Seeds are usually in fruit – the fruit is eaten by animals and the seeds dispersed in their droppings.

Understorey layer. Usually sparse because of the darkness, but dense where there are gaps in the higher layers. Some trees are of the same species as the taller trees, but are small due to the darkness.

Dark forest floor. Little vegetation. Some shrubs, herbs, and seedlings. Decomposing vegetation supports many fungi.

Soil

Thin litter layer – high temperatures and rainfall result in rapid breakdown and recycling of nutrients

Light colour – leaching has removed iron and aluminium compounds (they accumulate in the darker clay layer)

On *basic* rocks, the iron and aluminium compounds remain in a reddish upper horizon

Fig. 4 Tropical forest – the emergent trees can be very tall, reaching up to 60 metres

hamburgers in the USA has decreased as a result of cheap beef imports. But what are the effects on the exporting country? Summarise the arguments for and against clearing large areas of tropical forest for cattle ranching.

Forest destruction

Large areas of tropical forest still survive in almost their natural state, but more than half the forests have been cleared, and the pace of felling is rapid. The need to conserve wildlife and prevent soil erosion reminds us to be cautious about the destruction of the rainforest, though this has

to be balanced against the desperate need for farmland in areas of rapid population growth.

Figure 5 on p. 114 shows some of the reasons for the rapid destruction of the rainforest in Brazil. There are immense pressures on the government to go ahead with developing the area. Rich countries have made loans and investments to make these developments possible. Yet the damage to the environment of the Amazon and to the world environment will be on a frightening scale if it continues.

Where rainfall is seasonal, as in the monsoon areas of South-east Asia, deciduous trees are more common, so for part of the year light can penetrate down to

ground level. These regions support dense undergrowth, giving the true impenetrable 'jungle' of the story books. As in the evergreen forest, many of the trees are of great commercial importance. Teak, for example, is always in demand for making furniture.

---

5 Use the information on tropical forests to describe
  a two ways in which climate affects vegetation
  b one way in which climate affects soil.

DEVELOPMENT PRESSURES

leading to forest clearance

Flooding of the land for hydro-electric schemes

Clearing trees to make room for farming - often beef ranching, which employs few people but needs large areas

Roads and railways

Mineral exploitation

Settlements for people moving from crowded areas of Brazil

Tree felling for timber

Most of these trees are burnt, not used for timber

Fig. 5 The destruction of the Amazon rainforest. The photograph shows a tree-crusher at work. World-wide, an area the size of 40 football pitches is destroyed every minute, and in a year this adds up to an area the size of England and Wales

ENVIRONMENTAL RESULTS

Burning the trees releases carbon dioxide into the air. This results in a warming of the earth's atmosphere. In turn this may cause crops to fail in some parts of the world and low-lying areas throughout the world to be flooded

Fewer trees to absorb carbon dioxide from the air. This adds to the warming of the earth's atmosphere

Soil erosion

Loss of plant and animal species which might be useful for drugs and medicines

OTHER RESULTS

Loss of income for rubber tappers whose trees are destroyed

Loss of traditional way of life for Amazonian Indians

Wealth for companies and investors in development schemes

Temperate and coniferous forests

The natural vegetation

Large areas of the northern hemisphere – Canada, Scandinavia, and the northern parts of the former Soviet Union – are still covered by dense forest. The far north is too cold and dry for trees to survive, but if you travel south across the Arctic wastes you eventually come across a few dwarf birches and conifers. Further south still, the trees become so tall and grow so close together that little light reaches the ground. The trees are mostly evergreen, and careful use of the scarce supply of energy from weak sunlight allows them to keep their leaves for many years. The leaves are dark-coloured so that they absorb as much heat as possible, and they are long and thin, like needles. These trees – spruce (the most common), pine, fir, and larch (which loses its needles in winter) – are called *conifers* because their seed is contained in cones which come gradually to maturity over several years. They are well adapted to the snow, to the low winter temperatures (down to -40°C), and to the fact that for up to half the year the mois-

ture they need for growth is trapped in the frozen ground. This is the *boreal forest* or *taiga*.

Further south, where winters are shorter and sunshine more intense, broad-leaved deciduous trees are generally more successful than conifers except in cold, mountainous areas. Oak and beech trees, both deciduous, form typical climax vegetation in Britain, though conifers grow rapidly in Forestry Commission and private plantations and provide a useful source of timber and of wood pulp for paper making.

Deciduous trees, which lose their leaves in winter, rely on an adequate supply of moisture through the summer months. But further south, in the Mediterranean latitudes of Europe, there is a summer drought. Here conifers reappear, but unlike conifers in the boreal forest whose pointed tops easily shed snow, the Mediterranean conifers are often flat-topped.

In these southern latitudes frosts are rare, so the need to shed sappy leaves in winter disappears. Broad-leaved trees as well as conifers are evergreen. The olive and the evergreen oak both keep their leaves throughout the year.

In some southern areas of the USA it seems that pines are more common than

deciduous trees because they are better at surviving fire. Natural fires are caused by severe thunderstorms, and seedlings of oak and elm are easily destroyed. The buds of the young pine, on the other hand, are surrounded by thick tufts of long needles which burn at a low temperature and give the buds some protection. Another advantage is that their pulpy bark tends to scorch rather than burn.

6 Explain why
   a trees such as spruce are well adapted to short growing seasons and winter cold
   b deciduous trees need plenty of moisture during the summer months
   c evergreens are well-suited to areas with a Mediterranean climate.

The disappearing forest

A few thousand years ago almost all of Britain, apart from the highest and most rugged mountains and some marshy areas, was covered in forest. But today only 5% is woodland. Forests have sometimes disappeared because of the demand for timber, which has often been the raw material for houses, furniture, charcoal and ships. More often the trees were cleared to make

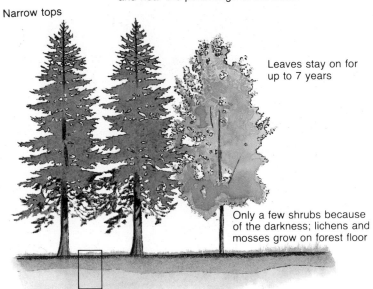

Deciduous trees such as birch, willow, and aspen are found at high altitudes and near the polar edge of the forest

Narrow tops

Leaves stay on for up to 7 years

Only a few shrubs because of the darkness; lichens and mosses grow on forest floor

Nuts and winged seeds are common (whereas most tropical trees have pulpy fruits)

Ivy, mosses, lichens, algae on tree trunks

Soil: podzol (see p.107) Soil frozen in winter, thawed in summer. Underlying rock may be permanently frozen (*permafrost*).

Height of trees. Varies with climate and species. The giant redwoods of the west coast of North America reach 100m. Most species only reach 20-25m, much less at high altitudes and near the polar edge of the forest.
Spacing. In the north, where winters are long, trees are separated by gaps. Further south they grow close together, often forming *stands* of the same species (useful for commercial forestry).

Fig. 6 The boreal forest

Soil: brown earth (see p. 107) Smaller loss of minerals by leaching than in podzols. Rich in soil fauna, so greater mixing of horizons.

Tree canopies are at approximately the same height – one layer rather than many (a contrast with the tropical forest).
Type of soil influences tree species: beech is common on thin chalk soils, ash on limestone, oak and elm on clay, willows and alder in poorly drained areas.

Fig. 7 The temperate forest

farmland. Forests mostly survived in areas of poor soil or where rich landowners wanted to keep them as hunting areas or simply for their beauty.

In more northerly areas such as Scandinavia there has been less pressure to create farmland because the climate is so harsh that trees are often the most profitable crop that can be grown. In remote places the forest survives in its natural state. Elsewhere vast areas have been felled for timber and for papermaking. At one time there was little replanting, but fortunately many forestry companies are now replacing felled trees with seedlings specially grown in 'tree nurseries'.

Forests are under threat from fire as well as from cutting. A carelessly thrown cigarette stub can destroy a forest that has taken hundreds or even thousands of years to reach its present state of maturity.

WHAT ARE THE ADVANTAGES OF KEEPING LEAVES THROUGHOUT THE YEAR IN COLD CLIMATES?
- Trees do not have to waste energy growing new leaves each year.
- Leaves can photosynthesise throughout the year. (In warmer latitudes, deciduous trees can take in all the energy they need in the summer, particularly with their much larger leaves.)

WHY DO TREES IN COLD CLIMATES HAVE NEEDLES RATHER THAN LARGE LEAVES?
- Long, thin needles are better at shedding snow. If too much snow gathered on the tree, branches would be torn off by the extra weight.

- The leaves of deciduous trees contain large amounts of sap and are killed if this freezes in the intense cold. The needles of coniferous trees contain little sap.
- The large leaves of deciduous trees have many stomata – tiny holes used to absorb carbon dioxide from the air and to get rid of oxygen. Water escapes from these stomata at the rate of several tonnes a day. In cold climates where the ground is frozen, there may be little moisture available for the tree roots, so this system cannot work. The needles of coniferous trees have only a few stomata and have a thick, waxy coat to reduce transpiration. If no water is available, some coniferous trees can close their stomata completely, though this stops photosynthesis as well as transpiration.

Fig. 8 Trees in cold climates

Fig. 9 Scenes of the East African savanna: zebra and wildebeest on the lush grass of the wet season, in the Maasai Mara Game Reserve, Kenya (above), and savanna grassland in the dry season, with a baobab showing signs of elephant damage (right)

Savanna

---

7 Describe the scene shown in Fig. 9. Why does this type of view attract large numbers of tourists to the savanna areas of East Africa?

Savanna vegetation is dominated by grasses. Trees may be entirely absent or quite common, but they never form a complete forest cover.

Influence of climate

Savanna vegetation is found between tropical rainforest and desert areas (Fig. 2, p. 111). There is no cold season, the major contrast being between a wet season and a dry season. Rainfall may be as low as 250 mm or as high as 1500 mm a year, mostly falling during summer thunderstorms. Grass can survive the winter drought whereas trees may only find enough moisture near rivers. The grass is dry and straw-coloured for much of the year but it grows rapidly when the rainy season arrives. Elephant grass can be up to 5 m high!

The trees of savanna areas are mostly *xerophytic* (drought resistant). The baobab is a good example. It may keep its leaves for only a few weeks so as to reduce transpiration, and its trunk, up to 10 m in diameter, can store vast quantities of water.

---

8 Refer to Fig. 2 on p. 111, and an atlas.
a Name one country in South America, two countries in East Africa, and two countries in West Africa that have large areas of savanna vegetation.
b Between what latitudes (north and south) is savanna vegetation found?

Influence of animals

The savanna has an animal population that is both large and varied. Patterns of feeding vary from one animal to another, which reduces the competition between them. For example, in the East African savanna, giraffes graze trees and bushes up to a height of about 5 m, while rhinoceroses feed on the leaves lower down. Short grasses are eaten by wildebeest, with zebra concentrating on the taller stems.

The huge number of grazing animals has a major impact on the vegetation. When a tree seedling is eaten it has little hope of recovery. But many grasses thrive on being nibbled and trodden underfoot – just think how well a lawn survives the constant attacks of a lawnmower! So the grasses and animals of the savanna support each other's survival.

Unfortunately, the balance of this ecosystem can be upset by human activity or by natural events such as droughts. Most of the large grazing animals (*herbivores*) migrate at the start of each dry season to areas where they will find water and grass. These migrations are spectacular, sometimes involving up to a million animals moving several hundred kilometres. But by the end of the dry season there may be little grass left and if the rains are delayed, overgrazing can result in long-term damage to both vegetation and soil.

Influence of soil

The dampness and nutritional value of the soil affect the type of vegetation that will grow. Many savanna soils are reddish-brown in colour, with a clayey texture. Sometimes they have a hard crust or contain rock-like lumps that are rich in iron. Humus is easily leached in the wet season, but fortunately insects called *termites* (which look rather like big ants) drag large quantities of vegetation underground and break it up, greatly improving the soil structure.

The pattern of vegetation in a savanna area often reflects quite small changes in the soil. Grasses dominate where the soil dries out for much of the year, but the proportion of trees increases where the soil holds more moisture.

Human influence

Savanna vegetation has been altered by cultivation and by the grazing of domesticated animals. But an even greater impact has been made by fires. Some scientists believe that large areas of savanna were once forest and that trees would grow again if they could be protected from fire. We have seen that grass survives grazing better than trees, and it also recovers more quickly after fires, though some trees such as the eucalyptus of the Australian savanna are adapted to survive fires.

Some fires occur naturally, the result of summer thunderstorms, but burning has been used deliberately for thousands of years. It gets rid of dead vegetation and encourages the growth of new blades of grass, giving more grazing for the animals. This is fine providing the burning is not too severe, but if the flames get out of control, serious damage is done to the vegetation, to wildlife, and even to the soil.

The savanna ecosystem has to be carefully managed if it is to preserve the features that have made it so popular for wildlife films and tourism. For example, the Ngorongoro Crater of Tanzania is famous for its herds of zebra, wildebeest, and antelopes, and for the lions that feed on them. Yet it faces many problems such as poaching (especially of black rhino), illegal grazing, and the pressure of farmers needing more land. It is now one of Africa's most carefully protected areas.

Mediterranean woodland and scrub

---

9 Study the figures for a typical Mediterranean climate (Palermo) on p. 101.
a What is the total rainfall in (i) November–February (ii) June–September?
b What is the temperature of (i) the coldest (ii) the hottest month?

Parts of Mediterranean Europe have a climax vegetation of evergreen trees, both broad-leaved and coniferous. But there are also virtually treeless areas. In parts of Croatia, for instance, the dazzling white limestone is almost bare of vegetation. Other areas have herbs and shrubs, but few trees.

The same is true in other areas of Mediterranean climate (Fig. 2, p. 111). This shrub vegetation has specific local names: *chaparral* in California, *maquis* and *garrigue* in southern France, and *mallee* in Australia (Fig. 10). Why should there be forest in some Mediterranean areas and only poor scrub vegetation in others?

Influence of climate

The climate permits both types of vegetation. Mediterranean trees survive the summer drought because they transpire less than the broad-leaved deciduous trees of cooler, damper latitudes. Many shrubs also have features that reduce transpiration. They have small, thick, leathery leaves which contain special oils (giving plants like thyme and sage a fragrant smell), and they can close their stomata during the heat of the day. Also, like the trees, they are usually evergreen, which allows them to continue their growth as soon as moisture is available. There are also *succulents* and *cacti*, which can store water in their leaves or their stem.

Overall, it seems that the shorter plants are even better at surviving the summer drought than the Mediterranean trees. Generally, trees are more common in the

Fig. 10 Mediterranean scrub vegetation

117

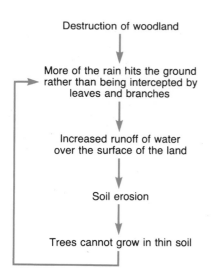

Destruction of woodland

↓

More of the rain hits the ground
rather than being intercepted by
leaves and branches

↓

Increased runoff of water
over the surface of the land

↓

Soil erosion

↓

Trees cannot grow in thin soil

Fig. 11 The destruction of woodland: the resulting soil erosion makes it hard to reverse the process

wetter areas, while scrub dominates drier regions, but the pattern is complicated by other factors which we will now consider.

Human influence

Scrub is probably the true climax vegetation in some dry, infertile areas. But there is evidence that trees were once more widespread than they are today. This change may have some natural causes, such as decreased rainfall since the Ice Age. But human impact on the ecosystem is just as important. Large areas of woodland have been felled, and every summer forest fires add to the destruction. For centuries, sheep and goats have grazed the hillsides, destroying young trees before they are large and woody enough to survive. Many areas of garrigue and maquis have a climate similar to neighbouring forested areas, but now have thin soils where nothing of any size will grow.

However, there are success stories of forests being re-established. Large areas of pine grow in the mountains of Cyprus as a result of an afforestation policy. Soil erosion has stopped and humus is very gradually being returned to the soil. And in

many countries around the Mediterranean the eucalyptus tree, a native of Australia, is proving successful. It has leaves which reduce transpiration. They are leathery and oily and during the day they can turn so that only their edge faces the sun. They also survive fires better than many of the trees that grow naturally in Mediterranean Europe and North Africa.

Influence of rock type and soil

These may sometimes explain why one area is wooded and another only has scrub vegetation. Rocks and soils that hold water will favour trees (if they are not used for cultivation). On the driest limestone areas garrigue often dominates. Here the plants are short and they are separated by patches of bare ground. There may be nothing larger than knee-high sage and rosemary mixed with bulbs such as the tulip, crocus, iris, and garlic. These areas are a mass of colour for brief periods in the spring and autumn, with periods of less activity in the winter (because of low temperatures) and in the summer drought.

On rocks other than limestone, or in areas with higher rainfall, maquis is more common. It forms dense thickets of shrubs up to 3 m high. Gorse, broom, rock roses, and tree heathers are common. Maquis may be climax vegetation in some areas (primary maquis) whereas elsewhere it has resulted from woodland clearance (Fig. 13).

10 Explain the following statements:
a 'Maquis vegetation may be (i) climax vegetation (ii) the result of human impact on the ecosystem.'
b 'Garrigue vegetation is mostly found in areas of (i) intense grazing by goats (ii) very dry climate (iii) limestone.'

Tropical deserts

The world's hot deserts are areas of low rainfall (less than 250 mm a year) and high evapotranspiration. Though nights are often cool, by the early afternoon the air temperature may be 40°C, the ground temperature 60°C, and the humidity very low indeed. The year's rain is usually concentrated in a few heavy showers, unpredictable in their timing and separated by periods of complete drought.

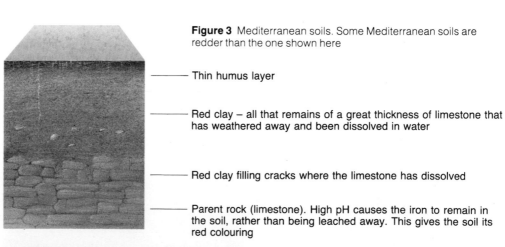

Figure 3 Mediterranean soils. Some Mediterranean soils are redder than the one shown here

— Thin humus layer

— Red clay – all that remains of a great thickness of limestone that has weathered away and been dissolved in water

— Red clay filling cracks where the limestone has dissolved

— Parent rock (limestone). High pH causes the iron to remain in the soil, rather than being leached away. This gives the soil its red colouring

Many different soils are found in Mediterranean areas. Deep brown earths have developed under forests. Thin gravelly or sandy soils are found where erosion has removed humus and fine particles. The terra rossa (red soil) lies between these extremes and is often found in depressions in limestone areas.

Fig. 12 Mediterranean soils: some are redder than the soil shown here

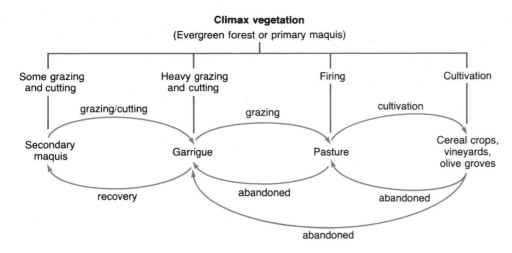

Fig. 13 Vegetation in Mediterranean countries

Fig. 14 Arizona, USA: not all deserts are sandy

How plants save water

Cacti are among the most spectacular water-saving plants of the desert. There are 2000 species, all coming originally from the Americas. Figure 15 shows how the giant Saguaro cactus survives the drought.

Other *xerophytic* (drought-resistant) plants have equally ingenious methods of saving water. The agave (a native of Mexico) has fleshy leaves (rather than the succulent stem of the cactus).

Some plants are *ephemeral* – they lie dormant as seeds until the rain comes. Then they manage to complete their entire life cycle (growth, flowering, and seed production) in only a few weeks. For a short time after rain there may be a carpet of flowers in an area that normally looks completely bare.

The leaves of the desert holly (USA) can give out salt so that they appear to be a whitish colour, reflecting the heat. The creosote bush (USA) has an incredible number of tiny roots that suck so much moisture from the ground that nothing else can grow nearby and compete with it.

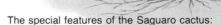

The special features of the Saguaro cactus:

● Stomata are in the bottom of grooves. Less exposed to the wind, so less transpiration

● Stomata can be closed during the day

● Leaves are reduced to spines (spines transpire less than leaves)

● Because it has evolved with spines rather than leaves, photosynthesis takes place instead through the green stem

● The stem is pleated. The pleats can expand after rain, taking in up to a tonne of water

● Thick cell walls which do not break when they dry out

● Shallow, spreading root system to catch as much water as possible. It does not rely on deep roots as there may be no water lower down

Fig. 15 The Saguaro cactus

The acacia has both a surface root system to obtain water from showers and a deep tap root penetrating to the level of ground water, as much as 7 m below the surface.

Water in rocks below the desert often contains large quantities of dissolved salt. *Halophytes* are plants that can survive on salty water, and they are common in deserts. The date palm is halophytic and flourishes in oases where ground water reaches the surface, and also along coastlines where sea water seeps inland.

Desertification

The spread of desert can be caused by people, rather than by natural drought. The process is called *desertification*. It is mainly due to people taking too much from the soil and not putting enough back. This can happen in four main ways:

- overcultivation of crops
- overgrazing of livestock
- bad irrigation
- deforestation (cutting down trees).

The chain of events involved in desertification is a vicious circle (Fig. 16).

The Sahel

The Sahel area of Africa (Fig. 17) is not always dry. Southern Niger, for example, has the same rainfall as London. The difference is that the rain falls almost entirely in three months of the year – and that the rainfall from year to year is very unreliable. Areas like this are called *semi-arid*. If the rain is to be of much use to crops it has to be held in the soil. Soils in Britain hold water easily. Soils in the Sahel are very sandy and generally hold very little water. When they are left bare after vegetation has been cut, they either blow away in the wind or bake hard like concrete.

---

11 Use the map (Fig. 17) and an atlas.
a Make a list of the countries that form the Sahel zone.
b Using the scale, estimate the length and width of the Sahel zone.

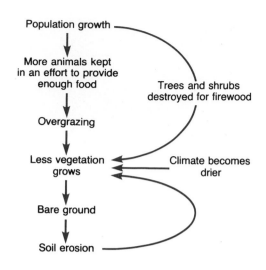

Fig. 16 Desertification

Traditional farming in the Sahel made the best use of the unreliable rainfall. Crops were grown only in the wetter south. The drier north was used for livestock. A number of different crops were grown to protect farmers against crop failure, but the basic priority was to grow millet or sorghum as food for the local community (*subsistence farming*). An extra crop, for cash, would only be grown if there was enough water. The soil would be cropped for four or five years and then left as scrubland for a fallow period of four or five years. Farmers in the south bartered and exchanged food with the nomadic herders of the north.

In the last 30 years this has changed. Population growth led to a demand for more food. Governments of Sahel countries wanted to sell crops abroad, so more emphasis was put on cash crops. Cropping spread into the drier, livestock areas of the north at a time when there were a few years of higher than average rainfall. Unsuitable irrigation schemes were set up, mainly for cash crops, and not enough fallow time was left between harvests. The crop yields soon went down as the soil became exhausted. Soil erosion followed.

Meanwhile, in the drier north, the nomadic herders had less ground on which to graze their cattle and sheep. Better con-

trol of animal diseases meant that the size of herds grew. Livestock ate pasture at a faster rate than it could grow. Damage to the vegetation meant that the loose sandy soil was free to be blown by the wind into dunes. The desert spread. Some governments tried to encourage herders to settle in villages. This led to cattle trampling soil and pasture around water-holes.

Irrigation can greatly increase the yield of crops in the Sahel. However, early schemes in Senegal were not drained properly. Irrigation water evaporated, leaving thick deposits of salt on the surface. Slow-moving water encouraged the spread of diseases like malaria and bilharzia.

The main source of fuel in the Sahel is wood. It is a valuable resource and there are often shortages. Many Sahel cities (like Ouagadougou in Burkina Faso) are surrounded by a treeless waste where cutting of trees for fuel has left the soil bare to the sun and wind.

---

12 Write brief notes on desertification in the Sahel under four headings:
Overcultivation, Overgrazing, Irrigation, Deforestation.

World attention was first focused on the problems of the Sahel during the great drought of 1968–73. It is estimated that between 100 000 and 250 000 people and between one-quarter and one-half of all the region's cattle died. A further million people were left destitute or totally reliant on food aid. As a result of the drought the United Nations made several attempts to help countries fighting desertification. A UN Conference on Desertification made a number of suggestions:

- *Discover local priorities.* For example, irrigation schemes that were waterlogged and clogged with salt could be improved. There were 20 000 ha of these in Senegal and Mali. Regional research centres could be set up, like the Sahel Institute at Bamako in Mali.
- *Each country should prepare a national plan.* Niger's plan was to emphasise the production of food rather than cash crops.

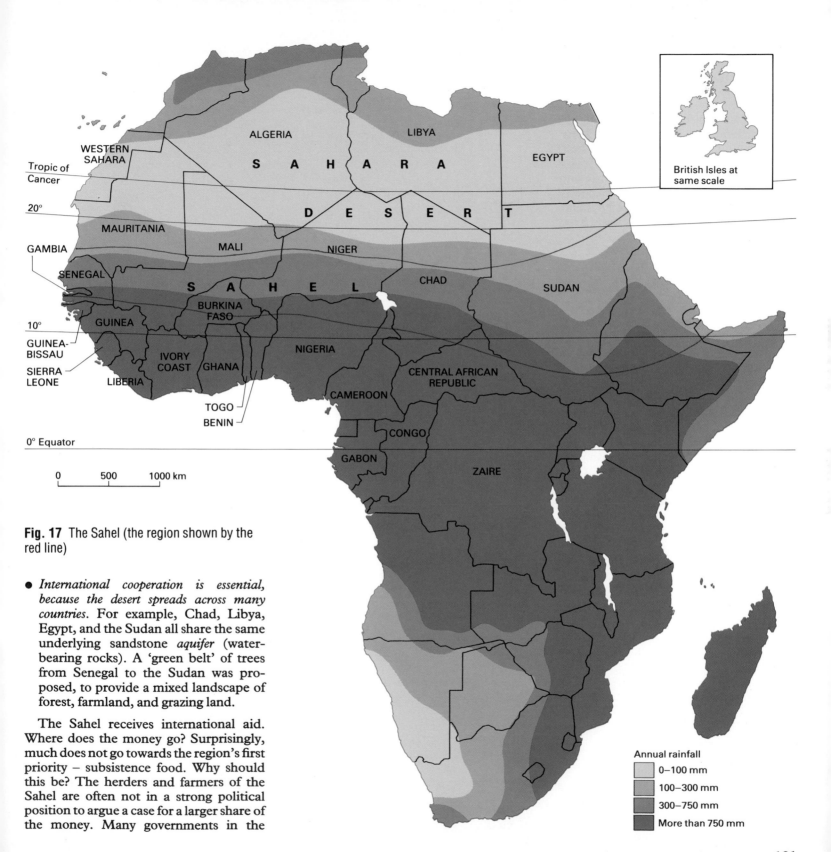

Fig. 17 The Sahel (the region shown by the red line)

- *International cooperation is essential, because the desert spreads across many countries.* For example, Chad, Libya, Egypt, and the Sudan all share the same underlying sandstone *aquifer* (water-bearing rocks). A 'green belt' of trees from Senegal to the Sudan was proposed, to provide a mixed landscape of forest, farmland, and grazing land.

The Sahel receives international aid. Where does the money go? Surprisingly, much does not go towards the region's first priority – subsistence food. Why should this be? The herders and farmers of the Sahel are often not in a strong political position to argue a case for a larger share of the money. Many governments in the

Annual rainfall
- 0–100 mm
- 100–300 mm
- 300–750 mm
- More than 750 mm

British Isles at same scale

Sahel have a policy of producing cheap food for the urban areas. This means that farmers cannot get a high enough price for their crops to make extra food production worthwhile. International aid is often in the form of projects like road building. These schemes are usually of some benefit, but many experts now think that the money might be better spent on direct help to farmers. In some areas governments spend large sums of money on weapons, and preventing the famine that goes with desertification has sometimes been a low priority.

---

13 Prepare notes for a class discussion on desertification under the following headings:
- How people make deserts
- How they could stop it
- Why they don't.
  Remember that there are different views on how to prevent the spread of deserts.

Desertification is an appropriate subject to end this book. It illustrates that people live in a very close relationship with their environment, and that this relationship is a delicate balance that is easily upset. Geographers working with other scientists are trying to understand the processes involved in this balance, and to suggest suitable solutions where the balance has been upset.

Index

Acknowledgements

The publishers would like to thank the following permission to reproduce photographs:

Aerofilms: 5, 33 *right*, 66 *top*, 67 *top*, 69, 75; Ardea: 82; K S Blake: 28 *bottom*; Bridgeman Art Library: 58; British Geological Society: 24 *top*; Bruce Coleman Ltd: 3 *right*, 80 *bottom*, 81, 83; Eye Ubiquitous/Paul Seheult: 88; Geoscience Features: 22, 49, 66, 80 *top*, 90 *bottom*, 104, 106, 107 *all*, 116 *all*; Geoslides: 80 *middle*; Hills Harris Photographers: 10 *top*; Hulton Deutsh Collection: 34 *all*; Impact Photos/Peter Menzel: 12; Institute of Geological Sciences: 10 *right*, 11, 13, 23 *top*, 24 *top*, Michael Jay Publications/Geopacks: 89 *all*; Eric Kay: 19 *top*, 25 bottom, 60, 67 *bottom*, 68 *top*, 73 *bottom right*; Keystone Press Agency: 34 *all*; Frank Lane Agency: 84/Roger Tideman 109/Steve McCutchean 119; Natural History Museum: 10 *right*, 11, 13, 23 *top*; Dr Simon Fowler: 31 *bottom*, 33 *left*; Photoair 47; Science Photo Library: 90 *top*, 97; The Scottish Highland Photo Library: 87; Martin Sookias: 89 *right*; South American Pictures: 114; Sporting Pictures: 23 *bottom*; Surrey Comet/Jeff Edwards: 43; Swiss National Tourist Office: 62 *right*; United States Geological Survey: 24 *bottom*, 25 *top*;

The cover photograph is reproduced by permission of Tony Stone/H Richard Johnston.
All other photos were provided by Ian Galbraith and Patrick Wiegand.
Parts of this book are based on material originally written by Patrick Wiegand.
Artwork by Gary Hincks, Jeff Edwards.

Whilst every effort has been made to contact copyright holders, it has not always been possible. We apologise for any infringement of copyright. If notified, the publishers will be pleased to rectify any omissions at the earliest opportunity.